Light Beyond Shadows

A Minister and Mental Health

R. Frederick West

New York

THE MACMILLAN COMPANY

1961

Second Printing, 1961

Library of Congress catalog card number: 59–7864

The Macmillan Company, New York
Brett-Macmillan Ltd., Galt, Ontario

Printed in the United States of America

Acknowledgments

The author is grateful for the generous aid of those who read the manuscript and who gave invaluable advice. I am especially indebted to Professor W. Wesley Shrader, of the Yale Divinity School, for the Foreword and for constantly reading the work and giving the original encouragement to write the book; to Mr. Darrell K. Wolfe, the Director of the Bethany Press, for friendly guidance and helpful suggestions; to Dr. John Paul Pack, Minister of the University Christian Church of Seattle, Washington; to Dr. James M. Kirtley of Crawfordsville, Indiana; to Chaplain Ernest E. Bruder, of St. Elizabeth's Hospital of Washington, D.C.; to Professor Charles F. Kemp and Dr. D. Ray Lindley, Vice President, of Texas Christian University; to Dr. Anton T. Boisen, the veteran of all mental hospital chaplains; to Superintendent Walter Sikes and Chaplain William R. Steininger of North Carolina State Hospital; to Dr. Richard C. Proctor, of Graylyn Hospital, Winston-Salem, North Carolina, for readings and counsel; to my wife, brothers, and Mr. Bennie O. Slaughter for reviews and accuracy; to Mrs. A. Miles Hughey, the State Librarian of North Carolina, and to her husband for literary criticisms; and, finally, to Miss Irene Elizabeth Yarbrough for typing all three drafts and for her unlimited assistance.

Light Beyond Shadows

THE MACMILLAN COMPANY
NEW YORK • CHICAGO
DALLAS • ATLANTA • SAN FRANCISCO
LONDON • MANILA

IN CANADA
BRETT-MACMILLAN LTD.
GALT, ONTARIO

DEDICATED IN GRATEFUL MEMORY
OF
THEIR HEALING ROLES

MY FAMILY

Mary Lewis West, my wife; and our children,
Mary Margaret, Rebecca Lynn, and
George Kenneth
The Rev. and Mrs. J. W. West, parents
The Rev. George D. West and the Rev. William G. West, brothers
Mr. and Mrs. Guy H. Lewis, parents-in-law

THE HILLYER MEMORIAL CHRISTIAN CHURCH

and especially
Miss Betty Yarbrough, Secretary
and
Five Official Board Chairmen
Mr. Howard M. Ellis
Mr. H. Glenn White
Mr. C. S. Tatum
Mr. John C. Rice
Mr. Laurie M. Rose

PSYCHIATRIST

Dr. Richard C. Proctor, Graylyn Hospital, Winston-Salem

CHAPLAIN

The Rev. William R. Steininger, State Hospital, Raleigh

Foreword

This is the remarkable personal account of a minister who in the prime of his life and ministry suffered a mental breakdown, and who, with the help of doctors, family, friends, and God, found his way back to a new life.

Dr. R. Frederick West is the beloved minister of the Hillyer Memorial Christian Church. It was during the third year of his ministry to this church that his collapse occurred. For a period of one year he was an inmate first in a private and then in a state mental institution. By some authorities his condition was held to be not simply serious, but hopeless.

During this long year of darkness his wife never lost heart, and his congregation kept his pulpit open for him. Once his return to sanity began, his recovery was rapid to the point of being spectacular. At last his discharge from the hospital was effected. He returned to the pulpit of the Hillyer Memorial Church, the very place his breakdown occurred. The road from this point was not easy. Many were the problems he faced as he attempted to fight his way back to a meaningful life and ministry. Overcoming one by one the heartbreaking obstacles that still threatened to destroy him, he at last achieved a greater ministry than he had known before his breakdown. Each year scores of hurt and baffled people, members of that growing fraternity "Breakdown Anonymous," seek his counsel and guidance.

This is a story that had to be told. Dr. West tells it with disarming frankness and candor.

WESLEY SHRADER

YALE DIVINITY SCHOOL
NEW HAVEN, CONNECTICUT

they stared like cold statues, gazing into empty space. They were ignored—and they seemed to ignore everyone else. I felt sorry for them, yet "closer" to them than to the others. I said to myself, "At least they are minding their own business, not bothering me or anyone else."

Then I noticed three men in overalls who were lying down. In fact, they were tied to their beds, their wrists being bound with leather straps. One man was screaming, straining at his bonds, crying for help. At intervals he begged for his mother as though he were a bewildered, little lost child—meek and pleading. Then he would act like an utterly different person, shrieking as if in agony and fear. At such times he jerked and twisted like an angry animal tied in a cage, but cursing like a madman. The second strapped victim appeared more docile, as though drunk and dazed, mumbling incoherently. And the third creature looked like a corpse.

I said to myself, "Perhaps he really is dead." Both fascinated and disturbed, I wondered: "Who are these pathetic creatures? What kind of place is this? A prison, no doubt!" At that moment someone unlocked the only door to let in an outsider. But the newcomer was dressed in white, which did not make sense to me. I observed: "If this really is a prison, it's no ordinary prison. The intruder wears no gun, and has no badge or club. Nevertheless, it is obvious that these tied men are being punished or disciplined."

I asked myself: "How can the folks in overalls seem so human, yet act so beastly? And why doesn't somebody do something to help the ones who are tied to their beds? Something mysterious and cruel is going on here."

While pondering, I noticed other types of people in the big room. They were all neatly dressed in white, and apparently well fed and comfortable. Some were men; the others were women. I thought: "Who are they? They look like doctors and nurses. If so, why are their patients dressed in overalls? Why not pajamas or street clothes?"

2

1

Strange Place, People, and Voices

One day I found myself in strange company. It was like waking during a horrible nightmare. Only, the weird dream really came true. It was that sudden and startling.

The place was a state mental hospital, but I did not know it. I was a patient, but unaware of it. The event occurred in late January, 1954. But I did not know that, either.

When I came to myself, I was in a huge long room. There were no pictures or decorations, but noise and confusion abounded. The unattractive room was outdated and dilapidated—more suitable for livestock than for human beings. But the room was crowded with people, standing around or near two rows of single beds, who looked even more curious and depressing than the drab room.

I saw more than a dozen thin, haggard, worn-out men. Nervous and drawn, they looked more like odd human wrecks than like normal human beings. All were crudely dressed alike—each man in overalls. "Farmers, no doubt," I thought.

Most of them seemed as excited as schoolchildren during recess. But some grinned too much and talked too loudly. Others laughed and laughed. I had the strange feeling that they were laughing at me. *Are they talking about me, too?* Their very gaiety made me feel all the more uncomfortable and out of place.

But a few were sad, silent, or sullen. Withdrawn from the others,

Preface

This book is a frank effort to share some personal impressions and experiences in regard to my own mental illness, recovery, and re-adjustments. It is written for former and potential patients, and for their relatives and friends. They know that I am a minister, not a doctor; and not an expert, but an ex-patient. Craving a personal story, they come to me with a mutual problem, like alcoholics, and their loved ones approach a witness like that within the Alcoholics Anonymous movement. My hope is that this book will be of wider help than these confidential chats.

This is neither a scientific treatise nor the self-study of a technical authority. I am more interested in the sick person than in the sick disease. To observe, study, and master such cases objectively is one thing; but to have been one yourself is quite another. One can study and analyze the sugar content of a grape. But you never know quite how bitter or sweet the grape actually tastes until you sample it yourself. That is why we former patients freely share what we feel and think with one another from our common personal experiences.

Mild "nervous breakdowns" are fashionable. As with psychiatrists, trips to Europe, and operations—if you haven't had one, you're not "up to date." However, my condition was critical, and I was in both private and state mental institutions. No one wants to be that "modern." Such serious illnesses are like rains from the heavens—falling upon the just and the unjust, the young and the aged, the educated and the uneducated, believers and skeptics, and upon the rich and the poor alike.

All places, names, and events in this story are real. For permission to quote our conversations, I am indebted to my wife, my father, and to Dr. Richard C. Proctor, Chaplain William R. Steininger, and Mr. Bennie O. Slaughter.

To readers who find it difficult to believe that all persons, patients and nonpatients, are human beings like themselves, I offer this, my personal story.

Contents

Contents

Light Beyond Shadows

This spectacle of variety and contrasts perplexed me. Now it appeared more likely that I was a visitor or spectator within a strange hospital. I debated: "If so, it's no ordinary hospital. Some secret, inhuman experiments are going on. An informed public would never stand for anything like this—even if the government itself were experimenting with volunteers to test the extremes of human endurance and survival. Maybe they are trying to improve training and supply techniques for future military programs. Or—another possibility—perhaps we are being persecuted even as the Jews were persecuted by the Nazi régime in Europe? If so, these are prisoners being tortured for conscience' sake. On the other hand, our American government may not be involved; this could be secret scientific research to advance medical science."

Finally, I became alarmed about my own plight. My body was rigid, and I felt depressed and horrified. My mind was racing. I asked myself: "What am I doing in a place like this? Why have I been especially invited to see this sad exhibition of suffering humanity? Am I on some commission to discover and to protest about what is going on? Or am I being used as a stooge to sanction this cruel and repulsive procedure?"

I furtively moved to the nearest window, hoping to get my bearings without anyone noticing me. Everything outside the window looked too much the same, and out of focus. Or perhaps my own vision was blurred and distorted. I decided to try my glasses. Reaching into my pockets, I found nothing. But I made an unbelievable discovery: "*I, too, am wearing overalls!* I am one of the victims myself!" Panic seized me. Then I discovered that my pocketbook was gone. "These inhuman rascals have robbed me!" I thought. "My wrist watch has been taken. Not even my handkerchief is left; and my pockets are empty. They must have drugged me!" Anger, fear and indignation inflamed me.

However, I soon calmed down, resolving to find out more about my stolen belongings later. Now my immediate goal was to find out

3

where I was. I grimly resolved: "They'll never get by with this trickery! I'll escape, once I get my bearings and make my plans." I looked out the window more carefully.

What a grim sight! I saw trees, grass, birds, clouds, and the sun— but no color or beauty anywhere. The whole world of nature seemed cold, barren, and hostile. I could see the outlines of things as a whole, but few details. Under closer scrutiny everything looked gray, dull, monotonous, drained of all beauty and warmth.

After a while I saw the dim outlines of a city on a high hill opposite our building. At first it was vague and unfamiliar; then, strangely familiar. "Can that be Raleigh?" I wondered, as I studied the skyline. "Yes, I'm sure it's the capital city of North Carolina. But how can that be? I'm a Virginian, not a Tarheel! Years ago, I played college basketball and tennis in North Carolina, but never at Raleigh. Somehow, I have known this place well, but why and when?"

In the midst of this debate, I heard strange voices. They were comforting, but distracting. They seemed especially intended for me; though they were close enough to sound near, they seemed far away. They sounded queer, and noisy; they were both annoying and enticing. Like broken records, they kept yelling and whispering, "Fred! Fred!" They all spoke at the same time—now there were many of them—and from as many different directions!

I refused to answer, thinking: "They don't have the courage to come out into the open, or any better manners than to try to talk to me all at the same time, so why should I reply? And suppose they are part of a secret scheme to make me talk and reveal my plan to escape! Such strategy might be typical of the clever brains controlling this subtle torture chamber. I shall not play into the hands of my enemies at any price!"

However, the strange voices became more convincing, reassuring, and confidential. They seemed so private, as though for me alone:

"Fred, get out of here! Escape! Take your time; use your head; plan carefully. You can fool them all! We'll help you. We have our plans; we are waiting for you to make yours. Nobody has a right to be so cruel to you. *You don't deserve to be locked up.* We know what they are up to, just as you do now."

The messages made sense, soothing my anxiety. I thought: "Wonderful! The word has leaked out about me, and organized outside help for escape is already at hand."

The voices became less vague and mysterious. They no longer came from all directions at once. Suddenly, only a single voice now spoke—the soft, familiar voice of my own mother. She repeated, over and over: "Your brothers will have a car waiting outside for you. Don't mind, for it will be hidden. Nobody else but they and you will know this secret. Wait for your best time, and make a quick break. Don't rush. No, George and Bill have not forgotten you! They will help you escape."

I rejoiced. "How clever! Those strange metallic voices are only smoke screens to give Mother a chance to communicate her personal message safely." But when her voice stopped, I was apprehensive, thinking, "Perhaps some guard or spy has walked too near her hiding place."

Finally, I heard my two brothers' voices. They vexed me at first, for both talked at the same time, but from opposite directions. It was so unlike George and Bill; they had good manners. Yet it might be their strategy to outsmart any enemy. An important secret like this must be safeguarded; they were risking enough anyway. They said: "Fred, we are here—so well hidden that even you cannot see us. All you've got to do is to plan your way out of that horrible building. We'll be waiting and we'll do all the rest."

Although puzzled, I felt more at ease. Their voices were too loud, and yet quiet and muffled. I thought: "Perhaps they have a hidden loudspeaker device nearby and are talking from a great distance.

5

This is an age of new inventions. If this torture chamber could use applied science to break the spirits and bodies of men, just causes like mine must use science too. Yes, we'll 'fight fire with fire.' "

Cautiously, I turned from the window. Satisfied, I decided: "No, the others have not heard my confidential voices, which are again silent. So far, so good; now to make my own plans!"

I reviewed the tragic men in overalls. No longer was I sure that they were all farmers. But they all looked sick—and mentally ill, at that. I told myself: "So this is the scheme of our enemies dressed in white—to break down men's health, morale, and finally their minds! They are trying this subtle barbarism on me, too. Is that why my left foot hurts so badly?"

Peering down, I saw that my left shoe was much too small, cramping my toes and arches. Although the pain was severe, I detested even more the undersized shoe. My right foot was comfortable; that shoe fitted. I reasoned, "This is a stage in a complex plan to force me to complain so that they can tie me and do what they want with me."

I looked down again. This time I saw that I was not wearing my usual low shoes, but high-top work shoes. And for the first time I noticed the color of my overalls. They were blue. I glanced at the other men's overalls; they were blue, too. I knew despair, as the full truth jolted me: "*I must be sick, too*—like the other men in blue overalls. I am neither a visitor nor guinea-pig. *I am a patient!*"

So that was why I felt so beaten and tired, so weak, shaking, and despairing! Stretching out my fingers, I marveled at how they trembled.

I rushed to the rest-room to see myself. Surely I did not look like those others in blue overalls. But I did! My face was pale, thin, and emaciated, with deep lines across my forehead and down my sunken cheeks. I was as haggard and worn out as the others in my ward— maybe worse! My eyes were too piercing and glassy. I had lost much weight.

To see, hear, and think became more tiring. In a cold sweat, I struggled back to my own bed. I lay down in distress. The shocking salty taste of my own tears alerted me further to my condition. I sensed that I was seriously ill, mentally and emotionally. This self-discovery frightened, yet relieved me. At least the vexing mystery had been solved: "I am no visitor or victim from the outside, but a sick patient who belongs here in the company of other sick men. This is no inhuman plot; it is for my own good. I want help—technical, scientific help—I need it desperately."

Knowing that I was so helpless and dependent, I felt much better and more secure. The squeezing pressure was gone. My little bleak world made sense. I remembered reading and hearing about how sick men were when they heard strange "voices" and when they were suspicious of everything and everyone else. Already sorrow for myself had vanished. And I did not feel so lonely any more.

I decided: "Even if I am this sick, I can get well again by doing my part as a patient. I have been all wrong—these doctors and nurses are my friends, not enemies in disguise. They are here to help, not hurt us. My job is to cooperate, not to escape." A sense of grim humor returned: "Boy, I'll bet you gave these medics a rough time before waking up to what your real score is!"

Humor soon melted under a burning sense of guilt and shame. Horrified, I thought: "Why was I so stupid? Why was I so suspicious of everybody? I distrusted my fellow patients whom I do not even know. Okay, I'll get acquainted with them as soon as I rest, and am able." I concluded, "They are strangers, but we should be friends. They can help me, too; they can tell me what is going on and what I should do. I'll get acquainted with those doctors and nurses, too."

Though I was weak, tired, and miserable, my heart had new-born hope—almost a song. The two mysterious worlds of nature and people were one now, making sense. Even the birds outside our building were singing—not just making noise to distract me.

Glancing through the window, I was thrilled. Colors began to clothe the once dull trees, the grass and clouds. Even the sunshine looked radiant, friendly, and colorful—and it no longer hurt and blinded my eyes. The bleak all-gray world had disappeared. The colors of grass, flowers, trees, and birds had a beauty and variety and a vividness that I had never experienced before. Birds, flying around the hospital grounds, seemed to have unusual grace, majesty, and freedom beyond description. I was grateful for this new, wonderful world of beauty, order, and people. Everything and everyone seemed to have a significant mission and job to do. And so did I; mine was to get well by doing my part, a part which I had to learn from the beginning.

I thought: "This must be Dix Hill, the State Hospital in Raleigh. How sick am I? How long have I been here? How did it all happen?" I knew my name, but little about myself. I could fondly recall my wife and three young children. I missed them, and wondered where they were and what they were doing. I wanted to see them so badly, but I didn't want them to see me in this condition. "If only I could hold them in my arms again!" was my crying desire.

Then my interest shifted to the past. "What was I last doing as an occupation—teaching or preaching?" I could remember my years as a professor at Texas Christian University in Forth Worth, and also at Wabash College in Indiana. They were pleasant memories. I recalled teaching later at Atlantic Christian College in Wilson, North Carolina. I remembered: "Yes, I have held a pastorate in Raleigh—but was I teaching or preaching before I blanked out? And under what circumstances?"

I thought no more. Though I was too tired to explore my discovery of a vast new personal world, I had staked my claim! All I wanted to do now was to sleep.

2

Leaving My Hostile Island

I awoke rested and relieved. It was a satisfying sleep: there had been no nightmares! And gone were the haunting dreams, head-aches, and forebodings.

Calmly I reviewed the strange trip from my old hostile island toward a new, friendly world. I now knew who I was and where I was. Although I did not realize why, I understood that I was pro-foundly ill, and needed help. Desperately I wanted that help. Furthermore, I was eager to explore my new world of reality. The next step was obvious: I must get acquainted with my fellow pa-tients. They could tell me what State Hospital ward we were in and what to expect.

However, indecision and panic struck again. Alarmed, I asked myself: "Why do I feel so strange? A new freshness and an old tiredness—and both at the same time. Why do I feel so old? By George, I can't even remember my own age! I was born in 1916. But what year is this? *How long did I sleep, anyhow?* For hours? Days? Or could it have been for years?"

The last possibility jolted me. But a returning sense of humor steadied me. "Am I to be like another old Rip Van Winkle? He had a nap for years. And when he woke up, he found that he was a generation behind his times. Now, at least, I know how he felt! Yet this ward hasn't changed. The patients and the room are the same!

Perhaps this really is the same day as the one on which I dozed off."

Finally, I made my decision. Without further speculation, I resolved: "Why bother with such questions now? Go ahead, Fred; get the first big job done! Get to know the patients. You must take the initiative. You've probably already slammed the door in their faces at every friendly gesture they've made!"

My first efforts failed. Silence followed every "Hello." Ignoring me, the patients seemed to regard me as even more peculiar than they. "Okay," I told myself. "They won't trust me. I don't blame them! I deserve their stares and silent treatment. Why should they accept me after the way I treated them when everything was so hazy and fuzzy?" Now I recalled how a few had tried to approach me with smiles and greetings, and how I had "glared" them into silence and retreat.

I thought: "I must change my strategy. Why not approach that little man who seems to be their leader? The more healthy-looking patients crowd around him. When he talks and jokes, they all listen. Why start with the herd if its leader might accept me first? Besides, he seems likeable. Perhaps he's the most influential patient in the whole ward."

I approached him. At first he ignored me. But after observing me with surprise and amusement, he gradually responded. I decided to put my cards on the table. I grinned, and remarked humbly: "Say, you seem to know the score around here! I don't. I must be the dumbest guy in the whole place. But I've finally figured out that this building is on Dix Hill, and that I'm a patient just like the rest of you." They all laughed and nodded, knowingly but sympathetically. The announcement of my self-discovery seemed important to them.

Encouraged, I kept talking directly to him: "How about helping me, if you don't mind? What's the scoop? What kind of ward is this? And what can I do to cooperate?"

To my joy, he warmed up. Widening his contagious grin, he made me the center of attention. With a rich slow drawl, and a speech pattern all his own, he replied, "Good! So you're coming round at last. Damned if you're not a good Joe after all! Mister, you been bad off—'way off your rocker. I was scairt that some patient wouldn't size you up right and might knock your head off—the way you been actin'!"

Shaking hands warmly, he introduced himself: "You can call me John." Soon he launched into what sounded like a prepared speech, but one that was sincere and authoritative. Actually, it was the same indoctrination talk which I later heard him give other incoming patients. I sensed that he was the acknowledged spokesman of the cooperative patients, as they moved their heads with emphasis and approval at John's comments.

"These here other guys can tell you, I put it to you straight. This makes twicet that I been here as a patient. I know the ropes. The first time I got discharged, I went off the beam agin. I'm what them head doctors and medics call a alkia-hol-lic myself. I got out of this bughouse and done okay the first time, until I left my family's tobac-ky farm—I'm a tobac-ky farmer myself. Most of the other guys in this ward are farmers theirselves or work in the country. Like myself, they ain't got much education—but they've got a lot more sense than most well folks knows."

He said that he had left the farm, only to "git hog-wild drunk." Then he had slipped back into his former tendencies: "Likker, hoboing, messing round with no-good women—and gambling over the whole damn' country. So Ma, she had 'em put me back in here agin."

John told me that he had "heard tell" that I was a Raleigh preacher "with a main-drag church, called a Christian Church, up on Hillsboro Street." He said I had "gone to pieces" while preaching a sermon in the pulpit. Kindly, he consoled me: "Us patients, we ain't goin' to hold 'at against you, Dr. West, 'cause you preach for a livin'. Every poo' soul hast to earn his keep some way! As I see it, though, most of us ain't exactly yo' type. Take myself, I don't go in

11

for no religion, churches, and preachers much, but I do believe in the good Lord myself. 'Cepting I figure the Lord ain't got no use for a character like me, who broke most all His commandments!"

With his coaching, I managed to identify my local pastorate as the Hillyer Memorial Christian Church. I could vaguely recall its building, office, and many names and faces. Thrilled at rediscovering this missing link from my past, I probed John about our ward, staff, and my role as a fellow patient.

He announced: "This here is the Male Insulin Ward in the Royster Building. Like you done said, it's Dix Hill. But you sho' got to learn to cooperate with the doctors and nurses real fast so you can git well, or they'll demote you to the 'strong room.' Dr. West, if you don't cooperate, you're dumb!"

He went on, proudly: "This here ward is the best ward in this whole damn' insane asylum! Yeah, we got the *best staff*, the *best food*, and the *best liberties* in this whole joint—and that goes for more than two thousand patients altogether. We're choic't patients —they think we can git well or they won't give us their best."

Especially he praised the attendants in our ward, stressing that all of them were "good Joes." He warned: "Some attendants in the strong room and 'em other bad wards for the craziest patients are mean and dumb—worst than the bad and meanest patients. If a patient don't cooperate with 'em, them attendants will break your bones and mash in your brains. Yeah, they will—then swear that 'twas jes' 'self-defense.' They gang together and sign papers and make it legal—in case they need to clear theirselves. Yeah, they will, if you resist! All of 'em ain't that way, but some hates your guts when you don't do what they say."

With other patients nodding, John urged me to cooperate and to do what our staff required—"like we did in the Army! It ain't much different." He explained: "The medics, nurses, and attendants are jes' doing what they're told and paid for to help git us well—to put good sense back in our heads agin so we can git outa this damn' insane asylum. Course, some Dix Hill medics are good docs; but most of 'em are mediocre or worst—young green punks and foreign-ars. If they was as good as average, they wouldn't work for State Hospital. The best head doctors go into private practice and business where they can salt away more dough and deal with a better class of folks. Mosta these here Dix Hill doctors is young, jes' gittin' experience so they can leave for the first good opening somewheres else. Or they's foreign-ars that the State hires cheap—cheaper than American doctors, who's any good, would consider."

"That all makes sense, John," I replied. "Now, tell me, what can I do to get along with our fellow patients?"

His eyes twinkling, he advised: "You stay away from 'em quiet and sullen Joes—jes' like the rest of us did you. Them's too sick to know what they do. Sometimes they git dangerous when you press 'em! All you got to do, Preacher, is to git to know the patients what's got 'nuff sense to talk, play cards, or have fun and joke. When a guy can't laugh, he's bad off—you leave him alone and he'll leave you alone! He jes' wants to be to hisself and his own worries. Truth is, most us other patients stick together like old Army buddies."

On the other hand, he pictured the cooperative friendly patients as one of the most exclusive little clubs or "gangs" in the world. "The only way you can belong to our circle is to be a patient yourself," was his definition of membership for this unique fraternity.

"The patients," he explained, "like each other and feel 'way closer to each other than they do to the staff. Next to themselves, the patients like the attendants best. Us patients feel closer to the attendants than to all the rest of the staff put together." He said that that was because the attendants gave the patients more time, talked their own language, joked with them, played card games, and treated the patients with more understanding and consideration than most of the rest of the staff did.

He boasted: "Why, the attendants even know our names! Mos' docs has to read our names on them cards on our beds and jes' act like they know us. We can tell when they're pretending, but they don't have enough sense to know we know!"

My new friend reported that, next to the attendants, the patients best liked and trusted the nurses. He exclaimed: "Why, some nurses are real human! Most of 'em's nice to us. The student nurses are the best, though. You see, they're learning on us. They ain't experienced enough yet to git that there professional-phony look like a rookie cop with his new badge, uniform, and gun. You wait, you'll learn! You git to spot that strut and look in some new young docs and nurses a mile off! But, in the long run, the older ones finally teach 'em student nurses to act cold and inhuman—like us patients ain't people, jes' cases!"

His last remarks were filled with bitterness. A chorus of biting "yeahs" from the other listeners reinforced John's observations.

Lowering his voice, John informed me about what he called the "grapevine system" within State Hospital. He boasted: "News leaks back to us key patients in nearly every ward—jes' like it did among the prisoners when I served time at State Prison." Chuckling, he confided: "Us patients know more about the stuff that really goes on behind these locked walls and on this whole damn' hill than the big shots or the superintendent who runs this here asylum. We git our news from folks that's more honest than those stooges that writes reports and lies to the big shots and head doctors."

He cautioned me, for my own good, that "jealousy, bitterness, and hard feelings 'mong the staff are part of this whole damn' Dix Hill system." John believed that these staff tensions involved conflicts and rivalry in regard to income, promotion, rank—the actual forces versus the official recognized authority and power. He warned me not to pay too much attention to titles and positions, "because some nurses and ordinary medical doctors, what ain't no head doctors at all, really run the whole show and works. Truth is, the big-shot head doctors git all the credit and publicity! Like in the outside world, it ain't what you know that counts, but who you know, if you want to git along here. You'll find out for yourself if you're smart and act dumb. Sooner or later, some of the staff will tell you. Yeah, they got their troubles too!"

"Thanks for the help, John," I responded. "Tell me, what are these insulin treatments like?"

"They's hell!" he snorted. With other patients agreeing emphatically, he described how the nurses wake you up about 5:00 A.M. to begin the treatments which are given five days each week. "But on Sattadays and Sundays we git a break, like soldiers on leave from battle. During the other five days, every treatment starts with your pulse being taken, heart checked, and nurses sticking you with needles. Brother, you feel like D-Day has done commenced—that is, if you was ever in service! After each deep shock treatment, which may or may not count as a coma, they fill you with glucose to keep you from dyin'. Then they almost pop your guts with canned orange juice filled with sugar. And if you don't git back your sense enough by then—and still feel drunk—a hot shower on top your head usually clears you up."

The patients roared with laughter as he observed: "These here deep shock treatments are so bad you won't mind taking them so much five days a week—jes' to see how good it is not to have to take them on Sattadays and Sundays! The treatments beat you down, knock you out like daid, so they can put your brains back right agin, as I size it up. The medics, what ought to know, say the reason you pass out and git a coma is that this here insulin eats all the sugar out of your blood so's you can't stay conscious no more." He concluded: "No matter how you hate those shocks, you do your part and co-operate! Every patient has to git credit for sixty comas—or you'll never git out of this hospital without some real pull!"

I realized that my induction ceremony was over when John waved his hands as though the company were dismissed. The other patients had listened with respect and dignity. As though participating in a ritual, they affirmed John's reports to be true. All volunteered that

15

they hated and feared the treatments, but cooperated nevertheless. One declared: "These shock treatments are my picture of Hell. You might read about Hell in the Bible, Preacher, but those guys what wrote the Bible did it too early to know what Hell really is!"

Although uneasy about the impending treatments, I was happy about my new status and friends in the ward. As they introduced themselves, they wished me well and congratulated me on "clearing up enough to learn the score." I felt that my first big step toward possible recovery had been taken. I had made the grade with my fellow patients, being accepted and trusted by them, although they called each other by their first names and always insisted upon calling me "Dr. West" or "Preacher." I saw that titles and vocations in the outside world were no barriers to full membership in this exclusive circle. Once for all, I decided to respect their codes and their rigid ethics, for I sensed that their rules and traditions were unbreakable if one's trusted membership and friendships were to survive.

This first briefing convinced me that my next step was to get to know the attendants well. They could tell me more, and guide me. Feeling better, I went back to bed. A new sense of security was emerging.

However, I soon began to distrust the staff anew, especially the doctors, although I never became suspicious of my fellow patients again. And I felt that the head nurse of our ward was too talkative, self-conscious, apologetic, and prissy. To me, she might "boss" the ward officially, but she was no real leader. I thought, "Perhaps she is merely a stooge who plays off both ends against the middle between patients and the higher staff under whom she serves." *

Apprehensive, I confirmed my fears by observing some doctors and nurses talking in a huddle and pointing toward various patients. Especially, they seemed to glance in my direction and whisper. Again I suspected a vicious personal plot. Vaguely, I reviewed my earlier feelings concerning a scheme to emasculate me. I resolved,

"If I can prevent it, they're not going to use deep insulin shock treatments or drugs as a pretense to destroy my manhood!"

When my old fears were at a new height, someone knocked on the door. After it was unlocked, a friendly newcomer in ordinary street clothes entered the ward. He had what seemed to be a genuine nonprofessional smile and courtesy. He appeared at ease, looking as natural and normal as our attendants. Cautiously, I wondered, "Will the other patients accept him?" Watching, I saw them relax, pleased and unusually respectful.

Then I recognized him. Here was someone I had known before! He was the chaplain, an esteemed friend with whom I had worked in the Raleigh Ministerial Association. To my embarrassment, I could not recall his last name, but felt sure that his first name was Bill.

After chats with the staff and with a few patients, calling each by name, he came over to me, smiling and jovial. I was thrilled but speechless. Gently and warmly, he greeted me, "Hello, Fred! I'm Bill Steininger, the chaplain here. Remember me? We're old friends! You look a lot better, Fred. How do you feel?"

How could I say it? I felt as if I were in Heaven! I was too happy and excited to speak clearly, tears filling my eyes. Here was someone who really knew me and who called me "Fred"! I replied, "Better now." And immediately, eagerly, I asked, "How's my wife? And the children?"

I was anxious to find out where they were, what they were doing, and how they felt about me. But I did not have to raise such detailed questions. He told me exactly what I wanted to know—no more and no less. He replied: "Wonderful! Mary and the children are fine, Fred. They are at your home at Hillcrest Road right here in Raleigh, waiting for you to get well. They know that you will get well, and are so happy that you'll be coming back home to live with them again just as soon as you recover. They miss you, Fred, and believe

17

in you. Haven't you seen Mary yet? She has been to see you, hasn't she?"

I shook my head negatively. He expressed surprise that my wife hadn't visited me yet, and assured me that she would be allowed to visit me within a few more days. Overjoyed, I felt better, and more secure.

But I felt compelled to confide my worst fears as well as hopes. "After all," I thought, "he is a personal friend and, by reputation, an able chaplain! Why not share my fears about being tricked under the pretense of deep insulin shock treatments until some doctor can secretly emasculate me? Why not tell him, too, about my undersized left shoe, and how it hurts me? And perhaps he can provide some stamps and writing materials. Yes, while I'm at it, I might as well tell him that I want some regular trousers so I can get out of these miserable overalls. And why not get his opinion concerning deep insulin shock therapy?"

Hesitating, I unburdened myself. Chaplain Steininger was kind and understanding, never surprised or indignant at anything I suspected or feared. He convinced me that there was no plot to emasculate me or to hurt anyone. Gently he assured me: "Fred, all you have to do is to cooperate fully with the staff, and they'll help you get well and on your feet again. You can do it, Fred! This hospital is to help you and all patients who come here."

He shared my serious concern that my shoe did not fit, and promised that he personally would see that my shoes were matched comfortably at once and that I would get stamps and writing materials soon. Briefly and simply, he explained his version of the series of deep insulin shock treatments so that they made sense to me.

I was grateful. Now I was ready with my key question. "How did I get here, anyway? What happened? I don't remember a thing about it. It's all blank to me!"

The chaplain explained that I had had a "bad nervous breakdown" and had become "seriously ill." He reported that on Sunday, November 8, 1953, I "went to pieces" while preaching in my pulpit at the Hillyer Memorial Christian Church in Raleigh. On the following Saturday, I had been taken to the private mental hospital, called Graylyn, at Winston-Salem. There I had been under the expert care of Dr. Richard Proctor for about two months. Finally, I had been brought to State Hospital about two weeks ago—about the middle of January, 1954—for deep insulin shock treatments to "guarantee possible full and permanent recovery" so that I "would not lapse back again." He stressed that originally I had liked the idea of coming to State Hospital and had understood the opportunity, but that I had now forgotten about it. I was relieved when he observed, "Such a blackout as yours is normal and natural for anybody in your condition."

This was all I needed to know now. As I thanked the chaplain for his help, the idea suddenly dawned on me: "Why bother about my blackout and loss of memory? It's not the problem I thought it was. Why, already I know my age. I'm thirty-eight. How could I have been so foolish as to be afraid that I was fifty or sixty years of age?" We shook hands, agreeing to talk more later about my condition. I promised him that, meanwhile, I would do my best to cooperate and to get well.

Long after Chaplain Steininger had gone, I felt the warmth of his parting handshake and the echo of his consoling and confident words. For the first time I felt like a free man. The door and building were locked, but never again did I resent this once-bitter fact.

Soon an attendant replaced my ill-fitting shoe. It was a small matter, but one that convinced me that I could always rely upon the chaplain, if I needed him urgently. In addition, this event won my respect and loyalty toward the head nurse of our ward, for she showed real enthusiasm and delight over my shoes being matched. From then on, I liked her and welcomed her personal interests and questions. Her concern and encouragement meant much to me.

Moreover, knowing that Mary would visit me soon boosted my morale and gave an immediate and exciting goal.

I now lost my fear of emasculation. I thought: "This false suspicion must be another evidence of how critically sick I am! It's bound to be a reappearing symptom of my illness—some tricky persecution complex too deep for me to overcome without technical help." I assumed that the chaplain was kind not to point these facts out, giving me a chance to discover this truth myself.

I concluded, "Okay, from now on, I'll not try to figure out the techniques and approaches of the staff—or even of Bill Steininger. That's a job for which they have the requisite technical training and skill. My job is not to study the staff, but to find out more about my own mysterious self while I learn my duties as a patient." Amused, I asked myself, "How dumb can you get, Fred? You yourself are your own biggest problem and worst enemy, not the staff. You've been just like a corpse wanting to embalm an undertaker!"

Immediately, I made up my mind to write to my wife and my two brothers. I felt that I must notify them that I was "clearing up" and finding myself again. I thought, "They deserve to know that I believe I can get well; and that, no matter how long it takes, I'll do my part gladly."

But writing was unexpectedly difficult. My mind was sluggish and tired; my fingers were unsteady. Each of many efforts produced only a few words—and then fatigue. The good news seemed too important to withhold from my family, or to delay sending indefinitely. I learned to pace myself to see the clumsy task through as a new major achievement. However, several days passed before I was able to complete my first letter to my wife—on Saturday night, January 30, 1954. I wrote:

New thrills, joy, and deep hope surge every time I get a message from you, Mary, or from the children! How I love to hear and keep up with the progress and love of you all. I am so thrilled also to receive so many Christmas, New Year's, and 'Get Well Wishes,' cards and notes especially from an unlimited number of church members, friends and others who help raise my hopes and trust beyond measure. And from the J. W. West family!

I keep re-reading your newsy and inspiring letters of the last couple of weeks. . . . I feel fine—most of the last six days about as fine and clear as ever. . . . I hear that I shall see you Monday with a visit. This is thrilling news!

I mentioned the visits from Chaplain Steininger and another staff member, commenting: "Both helped greatly by being kind and frank and gracious in showing my need to cooperate with the nurses, doctors, staff and patients. I'll concentrate upon the most constructive work I can from now on, to cooperate. I am sorry that I have been so unself-critical and have not done my own part as fully as I should at Winston-Salem and Dix Hill both." The letter ended, as follows: "I love you all. Fred." A postscript added, "Neatness in writing was never a skill of mine."

My little hostile island was vanishing. I was being led away from it, happy to surrender its false securities in order to continue the most eventful and adventuresome voyage of my life.

3

"My Chapter"

By Mary Lewis West

The bright sun could not dispel the icy terror in which my body and mind were gripped on the January morning that I went to the courthouse to sign commitment papers for my husband to enter the State Hospital at Raleigh. I answered questions in a fog of pain and despair. One final crushing blow was added to all the humiliation and unreality of what I was doing: the request that I direct the ambulance driver to bring the patient to the courthouse to allow the sheriff to sign appropriate papers. This I would never do—I would save him the possibility of such public attention.

Again I was foiled in my effort to make things easier and prevent further hurt. I thought back to the first fears I'd had that Fred was working too hard and worrying too much—to the many sleepless hours we'd spent as he tossed and turned, unable to sleep after a late counseling session or a church meeting which had not come up to his expectations.

The thought had never occurred to me that Fred would have a nervous breakdown, for I had often heard him say that overwork never caused one. He had always been able to sleep anywhere, any time, under any conditions. If he had often worried in the past, he had concealed it from me. But more and more I was plagued with

22

the feeling that all was not right—I feared a heart attack. On two occasions I persuaded him to have a medical check-up. After the second one he came home and said his doctor had told him not to let his wife talk him into having a heart attack.

During those months Fred was restless. He was in a constant whirl of activity. He filled his days and nights with work. Every problem seemed to take on the proportions of a grave crisis until a satisfactory solution could be reached—and some couldn't be solved. Then he couldn't sleep, and he often suffered severe chest pains, but always refused to let me call a doctor. On several occasions he woke me with the same moaning cry of agony, but always refused to tell the nature of the nightmares he suffered.

On our trip to the West Coast, Fred was his gay self most of the time during the day, but at night he slept little. He had an abnormal fear that we would have an accident and that I would be hurt. This was very unlike his usual easygoing manner. Hitherto he had always enjoyed traveling, when he could relax, with no anxieties over travel conditions, time schedules, or driving.

A few weeks before the trip he had rushed back to Raleigh from out of town and had played a hard tennis match in ninety-seven-degree heat. Before the match was completed, he collapsed on the court. As a result, he secured the doctor's permission to take a trip to fulfill his speaking engagement at an international convention only on the condition that he not do too much driving. But whether at the wheel or in the back seat, he drove every mile of the way. The trip did not bring him the needed rest and relaxation we had hoped for.

All my persuasive powers had not been able to keep Fred from fulfilling what he felt was a divine mission on that November Sunday ten weeks earlier. My first real warning of impending disaster had come early on Sunday morning when he asked me to drive him to the church. No matter how short the distance, he had always driven the car himself. This was strange; but it was even more shocking to see tears streaming down his face and to hear his anguished words: "Mary, I hate to hurt people, and today I'm afraid I must hurt some. Or, more possibly, I shall be hurt. I may even lose my life." So the nightmare was launched.

As he stood in the pulpit, at times preaching eloquently, and at others lapsing into personal narrative which had little meaning to the majority, I felt as though my body were being lashed with a whip. I sank lower into my seat, and a feeling of nausea flooded me— a feeling which was to plague me for weeks to come. Surely, I'd never be able to leave the church without help.

Then followed the long week when I tried to play ostrich, assuring myself that nothing was wrong. Yet deep inside I knew that everything was wrong; but I thought: "I'll wait a little longer. Fred will get himself under control. Surely he won't break down. I am the one with nerves—not Fred. He has helped too many others to overcome their own nervous tensions; surely he can save himself. But if he can't—where shall I turn for help?"

Chaplain Steininger of State Hospital came to my rescue. Through him, the doctors, and Fred's brothers and friends, Fred was finally entered in Graylyn.

Graylyn—how beautiful in its outward setting of peace! How comforting it had been to my strained nerves and emotions to hear the reassurances of doctors—and to leave with others the burden of indecision and turmoil and responsibility which had weighed so heavily upon me!

But even at Graylyn I had not been able to save Fred from treatment of which I knew he did not approve. After Fred had visited hospital patients, I had heard him say several times, "I would never sign for any member of my family to have electric shock treatments." At the time it had meant nothing to me. Our family had never had any nervous disorders—it couldn't happen to us. So, in spite of much persuasion on the part of the assistant doctor and my brothers-in-law, I refused to sign the paper giving permission for use of electric shock therapy. Hadn't I already failed Fred in his request that I not allow him to be hospitalized? Surely I could not do more against his will!

But as I opened the door upon my return from Graylyn, the phone was ringing. Dr. Proctor was persuasive but emphatic. I had to give my permission immediately, for delay might mean life or death. But during these long weeks of silence from Fred, the fear had been persistent: "Did I do the right thing? What does he think of me? Will he ever forgive me? I did to him what he had said he would never do to me."

After my trip to Graylyn to talk to Dr. Proctor and other members of the staff, it was good to settle down to family routine. Many friends had offered to stay with us at night, but I felt that the children had had too many changes and been exposed to too much unusual excitement, and would be better off to get back to our normal everyday life. It had not been unusual for Fred to be absent at mealtimes and in the evenings, because of the full schedule of work he had been carrying. I had been assured that after a few weeks, and then a vacation, Fred would be back at work. Gradually, the children relaxed, and happy smiles came back to their faces. But at the end of the first week, our medical report was not good. Because Fred had not shown any remarkable progress, the great flood of doubt and fear returned. There were so many phone calls and visits from friends who were trying to reassure me and at the same time find reassurance themselves. This role was one of the most difficult I had to sustain during the entire experience. I was in great need of someone to reassure me and to serve as go-between for the hospital, church, and family. Yet I was the only one who could do so.

Holidays during personal tragedy are always hard. It became obvious that we would not be enjoying Thanksgiving with our families in Virginia as planned. It would be a long, lonely day for us. But the Sunday-school class which Fred taught thought ahead to that. Together they planned and sent a bountiful Thanksgiving dinner—

from turkey to pumpkin pie. Since friends are as important as food on such occasions, one of the families came to eat with us. They were good friends, with children who were friends of ours, and it was a gay affair with only an undertone of sadness and loneliness for the one who was missing.

Thanksgiving over, we began thinking of Santa Claus. Kenneth wanted an electric train, and Mary Margaret and Becky wanted clothes for their tiny dolls. With enthusiasm, I bought patterns and materials for a complete wardrobe. But I found I often had difficulty threading the needle because my hand shook so, and it wasn't always easy to cut in a straight line. But I tackled those clothes as though my life depended on it. And possibly it did. Just so much tension and pressure can be endured, and then the breaking point comes. Mary Margaret still says that I should have entered the clothes in the state fair. Certainly they were the prettiest I had ever made. Added to the joy they gave two little girls on Christmas morning, they helped me over some of the most crucial weeks of my life.

The first real suggestion that Fred might have to be moved to a different hospital did not come from Dr. Proctor, but from another medical doctor. The intimation was very clear that his might be a hopeless case and that extreme measures might have to be taken. Alone in the house at the time, I was plunged into blackest despair. In addition, I had a feeling of real rebellion against a God who could be so unfair as to punish Fred in such a way. I felt he didn't deserve it. The thought of his living in abnormal circumstances for the rest of his life was more than I could stand and still love God, who, I felt, could change such a verdict. Over and over I thought: "Why couldn't he have died? He would have been so much better off! Death would have been more merciful for him and his family. Anything would be better than this verdict."

When I was again capable of rational thought, I kept telling myself, "Why should I believe this verdict?" Dr. Proctor had continued to tell me he would get well, but he wasn't sure how long it would

take. Fred happened to be one of a small minority who do not respond to electric shock therapy. But as fast as I regained my com-
posure, the nagging fear returned: "Perhaps Dr. Proctor isn't keeping his promise to tell me the truth at all times." Often, during the
long days and nights, I found myself on my knees pouring out my
heart and soul, asking for help and guidance in the many problems
that confronted me in regard to our family business affairs, Fred's
job, as well as the ever increasing concern and unhappiness of the
children. And often in the back of my mind was the thought, "If he
can't get well, don't leave him in this condition. Death would be an
easier adjustment."

The great sin of my very thoughts overwhelmed me when I attended the funeral of the husband of a friend. How ashamed I felt!
Here was death in its awful finality. I still had the life of my husband,
with all the hope and faith that life should give. And I had been
guilty of asking that that life be taken away. I had felt that I was
wiser than God—that God was punishing us as we didn't deserve.
Indeed, any punishment was not too much for me now.

But with the beautiful and comforting words of the funeral service, a peace came into my soul that I had not known for many
months. And with it came a spirit of real thanksgiving that my
husband still lived and that I could have the faith that someday he
would again resume his place in our household. The world had
suddenly become a happier place. From that day on, my thoughts
were not *if* Fred returns, but *when* Fred returns.

For the children Christmas without their daddy was much more
difficult than Thanksgiving had been. But a trip to their grand-
parents and happy times playing with cousins helped change the
monotony and lonely routine at home. But, "I wish Daddy were
here," could often be heard at even the most happy times. His name
was never omitted from their bedtime prayers, and God was often
also asked "to make Daddy well" during grace before meals. For me,
his absence created even more of an aching void, especially at home

27

But there was also the comfort of being with those who I knew were as deeply hurt by his absence as I.

Still bolstered by the faint hope that after the holidays Fred would be able to leave the hospital for a Florida vacation, it was with a spirit of anticipation that we returned home. Each morning, upon awaking, the thought of what had happened would flood over me and the old nausea would return. The sight of my African violets blooming brightly in the kitchen window never failed to help dispel this feeling of pain, and brought the hope that today perhaps the good news would come that Fred could be released.

In the meantime I had to keep busy with normal everyday affairs. My inability to eat or sleep soundly had caused me to lose twenty pounds. I was convinced, for the sake of my children and for that of the church, that I could not continue idly worrying. Because the president of our Christian Women's Fellowship had moved out of town, as vice president I was asked to fill the vacancy. I accepted the office with misgiving, but with the feeling that our church was being so good to us that I could not refuse to serve in any way they asked me. Being close to the work of the church and its leaders in this period of crisis helped me to see our family problem in better perspective. It helped to melt away much of my resentment toward persons who I felt had misjudged and had been a trial to my husband in the past. Never did I make a call on the aged and shut-ins during this time that I did not leave with a feeling of shame that I had pitied myself so much, when in truth I had so very much for which to thank God. By being active in the service of others, I found the best help to my own problems.

Our hope of an early Florida vacation was shattered one cold bleak January Monday. The long-awaited phone call came. Dr. Proctor's voice did not have its usual cheerfulness. "Mrs. West, we aren't doing any good. I've called State Hospital and made all arrangements. Please go to see the clerk of court, sign the commitment papers, and then go to the hospital for an interview. I'll send Fred in an ambulance, and that way you won't have to make the trip." The choice had been made. I'd waited too long to investigate private hospitals where the needed insulin treatment could be given.

But once more I would try to escape the seemingly inevitable. I'd call his brother. Surely he would see that I couldn't sign papers committing my husband to a state mental institution! But he agreed with Dr. Proctor that we had no choice. It was the end of the road. My world and that of our children had collapsed.

I had not insisited that I see Fred after Dr. Proctor had said it would be best that I wait. The words of one of Fred's loyal friends and admirers came back to haunt me. "Why don't you ask Dr. West what hospital he'd like to go to? I'll bet he would know what he should do." Again it was too late for that. I seemed to have been pushed into a decision as revolting to me as many others I had had to make in the past weeks.

Now I must put my name on the paper which would take away his freedom as a citizen and make him little more than a prisoner of the state, and which would entrust his physical and mental welfare to a great, impersonal organization of whose efficiency I had grave doubt. No greater anguish of soul or torture of mind could be imagined than that which I experienced in writing my signature on that document.

My appointment to see the social worker and to sign the necessary papers was on the morning before Fred was to arrive about noon. What longing I had to see him and talk to him! Dr. Proctor had assured me that Fred was willing to go to the hospital at Raleigh. If Fred had agreed, why couldn't I stay to see him? Ten weeks had been long without a visit or a letter. But again came that old doubt and fear—I had done so many things I felt Fred wouldn't have wanted done. Now if I stayed to see him, and if he asked me to take him home instead of putting him in the hospital, how could I refuse?

As the hour of noon approached, I drove down the winding side drive of the hospital. At the foot of the hill my heart almost broke as I passed the ambulance and recognized my husband's figure as he sat within. His face I could not see.

By nightfall, Raleigh was closed in by a storm of sleet and snow. But as the skies darkened and the wind blew outside, our little world inside became brighter and happier than it had been in many weeks. The children were in a gayer mood. "Daddy is in Raleigh, and soon we can go to see him and he can come home!" Their eyes sparkled as they made plans of what they would send him. Mary Margaret's first wish that we bring his soiled clothes home to launder could now be realized. Their happiness was not marred by my own doubts and fears and sense of calamity. But the chaplain's phone call saying that he had seen Fred and that he'd asked about me and the children quieted many of my fears.

It was a day to remember for a lifetime.

However, the happiness of the moment was fleeting. Reality could be denied for a time, but with the morning came a new day and new problems to be faced. New doctors had to be met, and there were new hospital routines and requirements to be learned.

Visiting a ward in a state mental institution is a chilling experience. I picked my way through mud and water caused by construction work and the previous day's storm. The cold gray exterior of State Hospital was no less cheerful than the small waiting room in which I found myself. I might have shut my eyes and pretended that I was in the average doctor's waiting room except for the constant jangling of keys as white-clothed attendants came and went. To my horror, each time the door was opened it was carefully locked again. Locked doors and barred windows I was not prepared for. With added force, the dreadfulness of what had happened numbed my very being.

The young doctor was friendly, and concerned for the welfare of Fred and of Fred's family. But he did not inspire in me any of the feeling of confidence and trust that I had always received at Graylyn.

About a week after Fred's arrival at State Hospital I received a phone call from a nurse, telling me I could come over to pick up his clothes that had been sent from Graylyn. I thanked her but told her I had already done so. She said I might like to talk to the doctor about Fred. Again I thanked her, but explained I had already done so and saw no reason to go back so soon. The conversation continued, and three times the nurse mentioned that I might like to talk to Fred's doctor. Finally I realized that she was trying to get a message through to me, yet could not speak it outright in her official capacity.

I immediately set out for State Hospital. No one can imagine how I dreaded the visit. My heart was pounding and my hands were shaking, for again I feared bad news. As I looked up at the barred windows of the gloomy building, I once more found it hard to realize that Fred belonged within those walls.

The young doctor seemed surprised to see me again, but he was quite cordial. In answer to my questions, he assured me that Fred was fine and that he was adjusting nicely to his new surroundings. He said that at the moment, Fred was at the movies. He asked when I had last seen him. Upon learning that it had been more than two months, he was greatly concerned and asked me to wait to let him find out if the three-week ruling could not be disregarded in this case. I waited and waited, growing more excited each quarter-hour. I was completely unprepared for a first meeting—almost frightened. What should I do and say? What would Fred be like? At long last the young doctor returned with a stricken look on his face, and in a tone of abject apology frankly told me he had been wrong. He had thought Dr. West was doing well but he had learned that my husband had had a setback five days ago and had been moved to another building by another doctor. He would investigate and report to me as soon as he could.

My panic knew no measure. I could not help admiring the young doctor for his honesty, and I was grateful for his genuine concern. But the feeling that Fred was no longer receiving the personal attention of a gifted psychiatrist, and the fact that even his whereabouts in the hospital was unknown to me, terrified me. Whom could I trust or turn to in such a large organization? Who would really care what became of Fred?

Immediately, my thoughts went to the chaplain who had befriended us in the beginning of Fred's illness and who had followed his progress at Graylyn with friendly concern. He had phoned to give me good news of Fred's condition upon arriving at State Hospital. Surely he would help. But Chaplain Steininger was visiting in the wards, and his secretary didn't know just when he would return. I settled down for a long wait. I would not leave until I had some definite news. My trust in the chaplain was not in vain. He listened attentively to my account. When I had finished, he gently told me not to worry. He said that he knew where Fred was and that he had visited him since his transfer. He could not give me the assurance that he was as well as when he first came from Graylyn; but he did assure me that all was being done that could be done, and that he was having the proper attention and medication to prepare him to enter the insulin ward of the Royster Building almost immediately. Once again the church through its chaplain had come to minister to me in an hour of great need.

There was at least hope in my heart as I left State Hospital, as well as gratitude for the kindness of a nurse who may have risked her job to help me, and for the help of a Christian chaplain who was serving in his own quiet way.

Slowly the days passed, and I heard unofficially that Fred had been transferred to the insulin ward in the Royster Building. I knew that these patients were supposed to have the best treatment from doctors and attendants and that there was a comparatively small number of them. Some of my tenseness vanished, and once more I began to think more constructively of the future. Increasingly, I felt that I should like to be doing something with my time to help Fred when he was well again. I knew that one of the things which had worried him most was his failure to write the books he had planned. How I should like to help him in this achievement! I decided to enroll in a typing class at a business school to learn the keyboard, and then to continue my practice at home. The routine of leaving home soon after the children each morning and of having a definite schedule to meet did much to restore my physical good health. Again I found that my initial desire to help another resulted in my own best medicine. My first lesson came on the morning of my long-awaited visit to Fred.

After three months what would Fred be like? Would he have changed in his physical appearance? Would he be aged? A dream I had had continued to come back to me. I had dreamed that I saw Fred and that his hair was white. Over and over, this sight haunted me. Had his suffering been that great?

How would he treat me? Would he resent all of the things I had had to do for his self-interest? Would he feel that I had not been true to the trust he had put in me not to have him hospitalized, not to consent to electric shock therapy? And he had said that if it should ever be necessary to have him treated by a psychiatrist, to engage one with an understanding of religious influences and problems. How far that was from a state institution! Would he be rational in his demands for future care, or would I once again have to turn my back on his cries for help? So much of the success or failure of the past three months and the future might depend on these few minutes! No one had told me what to do, how to act, what to say.

As I drove slowly up the drive to State Hospital, I felt helpless, and unequal to the task ahead. The joy of reunion was overshadowed by the immensity of my problem. I felt as though the weight of the world was on my shoulders, and as though the eyes of the world were on me as I walked to the door of the hospital.

4

When the Lord Became My Shepherd

On the night after I wrote Mary my first letter, I learned to see life as a whole. This facing of reality came from a lasting new focus and under an entirely different light. The salt of my own tears finally let me taste within my innermost being the bitterness of my self-pity. This enabled me to see myself, not as I had pretended or preferred to, but as I really was.

My new outlook came on Sunday, January 31, 1954, on the evening before my wife's first visit. This crisis also came before I had received my first insulin shock coma. However, encounters with patients, the chaplain, and other staff members, and written messages from relatives and friends, helped to pave the way for this crucial event. Prior to those friendly contacts, injections of Luminal and sodium Amytal had calmed and relaxed me sufficiently to enable me to discover that I was seriously ill at State Hospital.

That night, especially, I felt like a lost sheep, lonely and confused, in a lifting fog. Discouraged and depressed, I sat on my bed after our usual early supper. Profoundly I thought, "I myself—and no other person or thing—am my own worst enemy."

I wept bitterly. My myth of self-sufficiency, pride, perfectionism, and self-knowledge was completely shattered. I thought: "I have long been a baffling stranger to myself. The more I understand my unstable self, the less I resent and reject the other persons in this

34

hospital who now seem so essential to my own life and well-being. Yet the more I know them, the better I understand myself and my own condition. Why this cycle of cause and effect?"

I pondered: "I was wrong so many times, before I could accept these patients as my personal friends and the members of the staff as my helpers! Somehow, I must learn to see people as they really are, and not as I first labeled them. The more I understand those around me, the more fascinating they become—each as a complex and unique individual. To know them superficially, on the surface, is not to understand them at all. To generalize is to make them, at first, complete strangers—undesirable characters and 'screwballs'— if not personal enemies. My God, why do I do these foolish things? Why can't I rely upon my own judgment and point of view? Fred, you fool, you need help, and I mean real help!"

Prayer came to mind. But I did not plan to pray, being determined never to pray again. God seemed too vague and far off. Dimly, I recalled: "I have prayed often before, but God ignored my prayers and gave me up. God is against me. He was cruel to allow me to sink into such an environment as this ward. God is too busy to care about a person like me, who can no longer do the least thing for Him."

While in this mood, I recalled my former philosophy professor, Dr. Richard Sommerville. A recollection emerged from my memory of student days at Lynchburg College: The professor looked typically calm and steady. He was repeating a favorite sentence which I had often quoted from his lectures about the appreciation of paintings and art in his class in aesthetics: "*When you cast a judgment upon somebody else, you are also being judged yourself—you are being judged by your own capacity and ability to appreciate and understand!*" His voice was low and quiet. But his words kept echoing until they thundered repeatedly, louder and louder.

Alarmed, I asked myself, "Are these words merely his opinion?" Suddenly, it dawned upon me, "No, God is now speaking to me through my beloved professor's insight! Maybe I have been wrong

35

about God, after all. I've surely been wrong about all human beings lately."

And then, out of the depths of my being, the Scriptures spoke: "The plans of the mind belong to man, but the answer of the tongue is from the Lord. *All the ways of a man are pure in his own eyes, but the Lord weighs the spirit.*" I recognized the opening verses of the sixteenth chapter of Proverbs from the new Revised Standard Version of the Bible.*

Astounded, I decided, "God is speaking His word through these Scriptures especially to me in my condition now!" I was afraid. I remembered Isaiah and how God revealed Himself to him in the ancient temple. I confessed with the Hebrew prophet, "Woe is me! For I am lost; for I am a man of unclean lips, and I dwell in the midst of a people of unclean lips." But I refused to complete the sentence, for I could not say with Isaiah that "my eyes have seen the King, the Lord of hosts." Nor did I want to see God in a new light. Afraid that I would see God "high and lifted up," I told myself: "I am in no temple, but my ward does seem to shake at the foundations like Isaiah's temple. And I, too, cannot escape the Word of God Himself."

Soon, a single Bible verse came to my conscience, "The Lord sees not as man sees; man looks on the outward appearance, but the Lord looks on the heart." In excitement, I found myself praying, "O God, You Who are too holy for me to see and understand, show me what I look like in Your sight."

A terrifying silence followed. Gradually my memories of the distant past revived. I found myself reviewing some bitter and frustrating experiences of my early childhood and youth. Suddenly I could see my childhood like an open book. I felt that God Himself was holding the book for me, as I kept confessing to Him how profoundly

---

* Scriptural quotations are from the Revised Standard Version of the Bible, copyright 1946 and 1952 by the Division of Christian Education of the National Council of the Churches of Christ in the U.S.A., and are used by permission.

I had fallen short of the best convictions and highest purposes of my life.

The most humiliating memory involved my father, a minister. I thought: "How I really did hate and fear him when I was a child, as far back as I could ever remember! And how wrong I was! My suffering, which I had blamed upon Dad, came from my own inner weaknesses, not his. Now, for the first time, am I able to see how fortunate I really was to have him as a father. How mixed up I've been in my attitudes toward Dad! No wonder I cracked under later pressures."

I prayed: "O God, forgive me now. I was wrong to make up my mind never to forgive Dad—to blame him entirely for all his fits of temper, for resenting his not playing with me as other children's fathers did, and for those painful whippings when I disobeyed him, or when I defied him, detesting his sincere faith—and for defying his honest views about You, the Bible, and Your holy will. Dad measured up to his own faith and background better than I have to mine. He had fierce pressures from church problems, his family, and from his own sacrifices for causes which he backed with all his heart. No wonder I annoyed him at times! I must have seemed wild and irresponsible to him! I was too stubborn and proud to put myself in his place until now.

"Have mercy on me, O God, for I was wrong to misunderstand my father and to grow bitter at his good intentions and love according to my own self-pity and pride. So often, I really did deserve to be corrected! In Your sight, I now see him in a different light.

"I'll never pray for revenge again against anybody. I finally got my chance for what I had thought was revenge against Dad when I was in college. And, God, it turned my heart inside out; I've secretly hated myself ever since. Forgive me; I have sinned against my own father and family. I am not worthy of his love, much less Yours."

Reliving that crucial event all over again, I recalled how, as a child, I had prepared for it. For years, I had dreamed and schemed: "If I wait long enough, I'll get big and strong enough from athletics, work in the garden and mowing grass to dare Dad ever to strike or tongue-lash me again." I thought: "What joy and freedom I found in sports! So that's why, God, I turned so enthusiastically to sports. My reputation as an unusual fighter and competitor within my limits came from far more than a mere love of the games and contests such as I had assumed. Dad was no athlete—in sports, I felt free from what I regarded as his domination, bigotry, and intolerance. And I was more impatient with Dad than he ever was with me. In Your sight, I now see these things."

Before God, I reviewed that long-awaited day when I was a college freshman. Mother was away. Dad had ordered me to cook his daily fish—his favorite Eastern Shore diet. I explained that, in spite of my Boy Scout training, I could not cook sea food. Then Dad threatened me. "I'll never forget how he raised his voice and arm—coming at me—and how I got set for the fight that never came.

"J. T. Watson, Jr., our preacher's son and my best friend at the time, was there. He saw it all, too, even as You did, God. He begged me to try to cook the fish, but nothing could stop me. I was seeking just such an excuse as this—a showdown when I could feel innocent and justified enough. Dad did not touch me. Nor did I touch him. As he backed into a kitchen corner, I screamed: 'Hit me, Dad! Please, just touch me, and I'll beat you until you can't stand up. I'll tear you to pieces with my bare hands. You may not know it, but I've been waiting for this minute for years and years.'

"But Dad did not open his mouth. He looked petrified and hurt; I proudly assumed that it was only fear. I begged, 'Well, why don't you say something? Speak up! Yell at me once more—it'll be your last time! You'll never strike me again. You get by with your intolerance among pious prudes because they call you a character, but a man of God with real convictions. To your face, I call you a selfish fanatic and tyrant!'

"And, God, You know, above all, how rotten I felt while treating Dad like that! (Even my friend Watson understood and loved my father better than I did then; his face showed that he was ashamed of me, not Dad). For the first time, I saw fear and tears fill Dad's eyes. This time, I knew that Dad was really brokenhearted.

"Suddenly, I felt weak and helpless before him. It might have been different, had Dad said one word or moved a finger. But, God, I was hurt to see Dad look so hurt. When I felt that Dad was afraid, it frightened me and I was ashamed of him. At that moment, something was lost that had always been precious to me. With all of Dad's limitations, which I had wrongly hated, You know, God, that I had always admired him for his strength and for his moral and spiritual courage as a man—he was my ideal of a fighter who would not compromise, hold his peace, or mince any words over a real issue or principle. I was then shocked at him. Worse, still, I was shocked at, and ashamed of, myself. Standing there with victory in my hands, I pitied my own dad for the first time in my life.

"I had planned only to prove that I had, not more, but as much courage as he in the final test between us. But the awful truth jolted me: if Dad had touched me or spoken, I would have killed him with my own hands; and I knew it! I had not planned to go that far. But ever since then I have felt like a murderer.

"As the years went by, I was no longer afraid of Dad, but horribly afraid of myself and my own temper. I tried to rationalize, to convince myself that I was not afraid. But without success! I tried hard to cover up my haunting fear and guilt by an easygoing and happy-go-lucky manner. But I never got over that defeat deeply within—or the gnawing despair it left. I tried to erase the horrible memory, but could not. I got my freedom from Dad, but not from the price we both paid for it. God, forgive me now. I now see that my own inner weaknesses, not Dad's, were exposed that day. You know that I tried hard to make up for that experience with Dad, but he and I have never mentioned the subject again. I took him to ball games. We had great times and fun learning to enjoy many things together. These new ties made me happier, made my conscience feel better, on the surface; but I remained miserable within my soul. I now see that I wrongly thought I had to win back my own father. Yet, all my life he had been a faithful father to me, no matter how badly I treated and misunderstood him. He forgave me, but I could not forgive myself."

Sweat was streaming down my face, arms, and body. God seemed nearer than ever before, but very silent now.

Before Him, I recalled how I had always admired, yet envied, my two brothers, Bill and George. When I was young, I felt that they were too big and close to him for him to scold or beat. George went through college, and I never saw Dad touch him. He was twelve years older than I. Bill was only three years older than I, but I felt that he was protected from Dad by his serious physical illness when he was twelve to fifteen years of age. I had regarded Bill as the pet both of society and of my family.

"Bill got all the new suits; I wore his hand-me-downs. He got the good grades in school after his illness. But I felt that I was the one with the insatiable hunger and thirst after knowledge and the chance to think for myself." I prayed: "O God, You Who know all things and the deepest sins and secrets of my life, I am ashamed. For the first time I now see that much of my desire for learning and education was from the lust to try to whip Dad in a way that would seem more fair and respectable in my own sight and society's—to expose his self-educated prejudices. As for the false pride I built up, it was partly from my ambition to out-think my father and family. I wrongly assumed that I could rely upon my brains, not muscles, for personal authority and revenge. I wanted to prove, not improve, myself.

"You know how I struggled to forget these memories, but they were rooted so deeply in my faults that I could not face them or myself squarely. I have long been afraid of myself, but I preferred to think it was my fear of others, instead. You, Who alone know my heart, know I have tried to rationalize and justify myself. My envy, fear, pride, ambition, and jealousy have been more deceiving than I understand. Even when I proudly boasted about my two brothers, I regretted that they were better and more understanding with Dad and Mother than I was.

"As long as I can remember, I always resented Mother's criticisms and remarks before visitors about how she had wanted her third child to be a girl, not a boy. I always felt that I was an unwanted intruder in our family, and not really belonging to it by choice or love. Yet now I understand, for I myself know how it was to crave a sister in the family. I have never known a more unselfish mother than mine, or one more kind to neighbors and people in need and distress. Forgive me, O God, for failing to understand and appreciate my own parents and brothers. I have really been rich in love from my own family, when I falsely felt I was neglected. Now I see that they have been good and patient with me, but I refused to realize it before because of my bitter rebellions."

Finally, I asked myself: "How can even God understand? He is so silent now. I am not worthy of His forgiveness. But—if He would only understand!"

It was in this mood of dismay, defeat, and doubt that I heard the attendants announce: "Bedtime, fellows! Okay, you guys, get to bed. Lights out!" I became aware again of the noise and chatter within our ward.

Feeling so unworthy, even of God's help at that time, I took off my clothes to prepare for the night. I went to bed naked—convinced that only Almighty God could help me now when I needed it most. I would not be tempted to conceal anything from His search of my whole life. I decided, "Maybe God is trying to find and show me my soul—if I have one left—if I have not destroyed it."

I shared and repeated these confessions—and other frustrating experiences from my childhood throughout my entire career. I prayed until daybreak, reviewing the sins and disappointments of my life, from boyhood until my nervous breakdown.

One other crucial experience, especially, I reviewed in detail. I remembered the public school teacher whom I had hated ever since I flunked the last half of the fourth grade. It was in my home town of Lynchburg, Virginia. She had me expelled from the West End Public School. And it all happened over the Lord's Prayer. The custom was for the public schools to open officially for classes at 9:00 A.M. daily. But we students had to be present fifteen minutes earlier while the home-room rolls were checked and religious devotions observed. She made us repeat the Lord's Prayer daily in her home room.

That day, she called me to the front of the class after the Lord's Prayer was repeated in unison. She asked, "Fred West, why didn't you say the Lord's Prayer like all the rest of the children?"

I replied, "I got all mixed up and forgot it, ma'am." But I did not tell her that I had kept my head reverently bowed and my eyes closed, as I had been taught to do at home and at Sunday school. Nor did I tell her how much those traditions meant to me. She cried: "Forget the Lord's Prayer? And you a preacher's son? Fred West, you ought to be whipped. How impious! Aren't you afraid God will strike you dead? Don't you know God might send you to burn in Hell forever for this? Now stand up here like a good boy and repeat the Lord's Prayer for the whole class to hear."

My memory really went blank then. I was frightened. I had never given a personal recital in public, and the Lord's Prayer had always meant something very personal to me. The more she ordered me to "say the Lord's Prayer," the less I could remember of it. In addition, I bitterly resented her order to "repeat the Lord's Prayer," for I had been taught to believe that genuine prayer had to be voluntary and prayed, not repeated. But I could not express my convictions. Then an idea struck me. Bitterly, I asked, "Say, Miss ———, what were you doing with your eyes open? How did you know that I wasn't praying the Lord's Prayer? How reverent were you? And what makes you think God would make anybody burn in Hell forever? I couldn't pray to such a Creature!"

The class giggled and laughed, but the teacher got angry. She took me to the principal's office. He believed only her side of the story, and whipped me. Then he sent me home with a note from my teacher informing my parents that I was "guilty of the worst impiety and infidelity, disdaining the Lord's own Prayer and showing disrespect for the authority both of God and of his human elders." Mother would not listen to my side of the story either.

In the presence of God, this vivid memory deepened my sense of guilt. I confessed: "O God, You Who alone really know my soul, I now see my injustice to others for the first time. Even as an ordained minister of Christ's Gospel, I have shunned the truth and scorned the sincere convictions and good in others' lives again and again. I have seen my Dad's early threats and violence in every angry opponent's face. Every lie and unfair attack made by my opponents secretly reminded me of that teacher and the misery she caused me. I have hated, when I was commissioned to love as Christ loved. I was about ten years old then, but at times I have acted like that same child as a teacher and minister. In my pastorate I hated my critics—as though they were scheming to win my parents to their sides in all controversies and attacks. I have sinned to the depths of my soul—against them and You, and against my better self, which grew so spiritually unstable. Forgive me, O God, forgive me now!"

Finally, my prayers of confession and repentance turned into thanksgiving and praise to God for allowing my present brokenness of mind, spirit, and body. No longer did I regard God as cruel, but as good and kind to grant such an experience to me. I told God: "Only in this condition could my eyes now be opened to Your goodness, mercy, and wisdom. Now, as never before, I understand clearly my own sinfulness. No longer shall I rebel against You and Your love. Even in my most sincere commitments to champion the cause of the poor, the wayward, and to bring justice and freedom to the wronged in the name of Christ, I was also championing my own personal cause and suffering in life. My passion for democracy in both church and academic life was stained by my own self-love and self-pity. In self-righteousness, I often identified my role with that of Jesus Christ and His unique mission as the suffering and redeeming Saviour and Lord of life. Forgive me, O God, for my self-idolatry, and for soiling Christ's Holy Universal Church with my own lust for power, popularity, prestige, and revenge."

My prayers lasted all night. I lay for hours in a cold sweat that soaked the bed coverings and my naked body.

The climax to this experience came when God Himself seemed nearer and more real than ever before. I could sense His compassion. Suddenly, I no longer felt weary, exhausted, and wretched. His holiness overwhelmed me. And His understanding love comforted me.

This comfort came as I was praying: "Create in me a clean heart and a sound mind, O God, You Who love even the most wretched, sick, and wayward of all Your children. Put a new and right spirit within me—come illness, come recovery; come death, come years more of life; come Hell or come Heaven. To have You near me is all that matters any more." I repeated the old spiritual with a new depth of feeling and conviction: " 'It ain't my sister nor my brother; but it's me, O God, standing'—no, lying down helpless before You— 'in the need of prayer.' "

No longer was I thinking of God mainly as the Creator, Judge, and Redeemer of mankind—but as my Creator, my Judge, and my Redeemer, intensely personal and holy beyond all human or Biblical descriptions and theories I had previously encountered. God became all the more real because He came to me as the supreme reality, measure, and meaning of all life, including my own. In awe, I thought: "Throughout my life God has never argued. He has always acted. He has given me freedom even to be a slave to my own self-centeredness. He has always loved when I have hated. He was silent even when I cried out against Him and against all His world and creatures. In His silence He always spoke to me; but I have often listened only to my own voice. He has understood me all the time, even when I have not understood myself, much less His other children and their rightful places before His holy Son. Everything else may change, but God is infinite, pure, and unchangeable."

I found myself repeating the Twenty-third Psalm. I repeated its phrases—meditating about its imagery—until I was unconsciously praying the psalm. Never before had I thought of it as a prayer, but only as a great hymn and as profound poetry. Nor had I ever considered God actually as *my* Shepherd before, but as humanity's Shepherd.

I pondered: "Strange, but I have never felt so fully identified with the rest of mankind before, including my own family. The Lord really is my Shepherd—with Him I shall not lack anything worth knowing and sharing that really matters in life. He is too big and too great and too wonderful to be only my Shepherd; God is everybody else's Shepherd too—even those who do not know Him as their Shepherd. From now on, *the Lord not only is to be my Shepherd, but He only is to be my Shepherd.* And I shall be a real member of His flock—even if it is merely in our little ward in this hospital."

Soon I was praying the Lord's Prayer as never before. I moved naturally from the Twenty-third Psalm to the Lord's Prayer, which made God all the more real to me as a Shepherd on His own terms, not mine, through Jesus Christ, Who seeks to find and redeem His lost sheep.

A new peace, joy, and gratitude entered my life. Prayers of confession, thanksgiving, and praise intermingled with prayers of petition. I did not ask anything more for myself, except to know God's love as a Shepherd and to keep knowing it. But I prayed that my wife, children, parents, brothers, and all my friends—and even my critics—might know the grace and joy of the Lord as their own Shepherd, too.

Then I prayed for the patients in our ward and hospital. I asked for their full recovery, but not for my own. I thanked God for "more blessings in this miserable ward than I ever appreciated or deserved in the outside world. It is worth remaining sick forever, if needs be, O God, to stay conscious of this new and wonderful truth." I praised God for His glory and love as revealed in the care of the hospitals, and the provision of scientific skills and of specialists to lead us human beings to a fuller, richer, and more understanding personal and social life. I thanked God for our staff.

I promised God that if I ever got back into normal society, I would leave it to Him to reap the harvest of the seed He has sown in all human lives in His own good time and way, even if it took forever. I vowed: "No more will I demand tests and results to see the harvest in other lives for myself. It will be enough to know that the Good Shepherd looks after all His sheep and ever sows for greener pastures and leads souls toward less turbulent waters."

Finally, I confessed, "O God, while I was too blind to know where I was or Who You really are, You were sharing Your gifts for mankind with us patients through this hospital to help the helpless. For this new focus and light to know and understand this amazing truth that was too big for me to see before now, I marvel! Keep, O God, this new light shining within me so that I can forever depend upon Thee as my Shepherd."

Then God spoke to me, softly and tenderly, but firmly. No longer did His voice seem to thunder as it had earlier when I was so frightened. Out of the quiet depths of my inner being, I heard God say: "You have suffered enough; but now, if need be, you will have the strength to suffer even more. Remember this when you deal with other people. They may be suffering more than either you or they will ever know. From now on, you leave the world to Me, My child. It is My world to run. Don't ever try to take My place again! Serve in the love of Christ, and leave your enemies to Me. Leave your family to Me, and your friends, too. Your task is to help sow the

46

seed of the Gospel and mercy, but it is My task—and Mine only—to reap the ultimate harvest throughout all eternity. I alone can bring order out of chaos, goodness out of evil, justice out of injustice, and mercy even unto the unmerciful. Have faith, My child, and My peace is yours."

God had spoken. I had listened. And I felt that God would have me sleep in peace. I felt that the deep sores of my soul and mind had been healed. "The scars," I thought, "may remain, but the personal hurt, loneliness, and bitterness are gone. I now love my brothers without reservation. I see my critics and enemies in a new light. Has God performed a miracle? Has God's grace already pieced together again the broken fragments of my spirit and mind? Surely only God, as a Shepherd Who really knows and loves His most erring and errant sheep, could do this mysterious thing!"

In awe and reverence, I concluded: "Now the good Shepherd has found me and claimed me as one of His own. I am no longer a hopeless case. I have recognized His voice."

Truly, the Lord had become my Shepherd.

5

A Touch of Home

My wife's first visit was on Monday afternoon, February 1, 1954.
To my surprise, this was a major event for our whole ward. The news
had spread over the grapevine. Patients informed me of the date
before the staff or Mary's letters did.

I was excited. I had not seen Mary for over ten weeks. They had
seemed like years. Her impending arrival was a major topic of conversation. For hours ahead of time, patients asked: "What does she
look like, Doc? Is she pretty? Is it true that she really loves you, and
cares enough to visit you?"

One patient asked, "What kind of car does your wife drive?"

"A 1950 gray Chevrolet two-door sedan," I replied.

Upon receiving that information, some patients posted themselves at windows next to the road during lunch and for hours before
she arrived. From their lookouts they studied every approaching car,
explaining that they were merely "killing time." One remarked, "But
if we happen to see your wife coming, we'll let you know."

Meanwhile, I was undergoing an inner battle. I was eager, yet
afraid, to see Mary. I asked myself: "Will I cry with joy at first meeting her? Or will I break down like a baby in self-pity? What will she
think when she sees my worn-out condition, the lines in my face?
Will it upset her to see how tired I look? I can scarcely bear to look
at myself in the mirror. How much harder will it be for her?"

I also wondered: "What will Mary look like? Will she be relaxed and happy to see me? Or will she be tense and drawn, as she was after our babies were born? Will she look as heartbroken as she did when I could not get the house she wanted? Suppose she says: 'I told you so, Fred. You never should have taken those teaching jobs. You liked them! But you should have considered me and our years of training to work together in a pastorate!' "

Another thought disturbed me: "Suppose she gets panicky at the looks of this repulsive Royster Building and ward. And how will she feel about my being in the company of these pathetic-looking patients? Will these sights shock her?"

The joy and interest of my fellow patients over Mary's expected visit gave me more confidence. A chat with a nurse also encouraged me. She said: "I have never seen such a complete change in a patient so suddenly. Why, Dr. West, a few days ago you were one of the most defiant and stubborn patients I ever saw. No injections of insulin ever so much as put you to sleep until today. For days you were so determined not to cooperate that you fought off sleep from amounts of insulin that would black out almost any patient. Your wife will be proud of you, and I know you will enjoy seeing her."

I said, "Thanks. Have I had any comas yet?"

"No," she replied, "but you will soon. You see, during the first days in this ward we experiment with small doses to discover how much insulin it takes to induce coma, without taking unnecessary risks. You're already one of the most cooperative patients that I've ever seen. Your rapid improvement is mysterious. You seem like a different person even since yesterday. What happened?"

I grinned, but did not answer, having decided not to tell anyone about my moral and religious encounter of the previous night. I felt that my experience was too personal to convince others. And my clearing-up period had been obvious for days, anyway. Looking at the nurse, I thought: "If I describe last night's struggles to the staff, they'll interpret the crisis as a sign of religious fanaticism or as a further symptom of my illness. If I ever hope to get released from this hospital, I'd better be mum. I won't tell the patients, either; I might sound too much like a preacher to them. And the same goes for Mary and my relatives. This is a private matter. I don't relish people who talk about their piety, and I don't want anybody to think I'm 'preaching.' "

I questioned myself: "As far as that goes, how do I know whether I am fully recovered yet or not? But who could know so soon? I feel as if I were, but I'm still fatigued, shaky, and run down. I notice that the sickest men in this ward are the very ones who claim they are well, and who tend to assume that everyone else is sick except themselves. I may not need these deep insulin shock treatments; yet I may, for insurance. They may help me to maintain these new insights and make my peace of mind and faith durable. Anyhow, if I return to normal society, it should be on the same basis as that of all the other patients. It should come as a result of objective tests which qualified specialists make on the basis of scientific and medical standards."

At last there was action at the front windows. A friend yelled: "Doc, here comes your wife! She's in the car you told us about."

From their vantage points the happy patients gave a running commentary on her driving, parking, and arrival at the entrance downstairs. Within a few minutes, the head nurse of our ward announced: "Dr. West, your wife is waiting to see you. You may go out in the hall and visit with her, if you like."

Somehow, as the door was unlocked for me to leave the room, I knew that I was ready for the occasion. Before I saw Mary, I knew that I would have control of myself without breaking down emotionally.

At first, neither of us said a word. We met and greeted each other with a kiss. Then we merely looked at each other.

Mary looked pretty; she was more beautiful than ever. Though she appeared to have lost weight, she seemed strong and healthy. She was so happy and relaxed that she made me wonder why I had ever worried about her reaction to my illness. She did not appear to notice my run-down condition.

She said, "Fred, it's wonderful to see you! I hear you're making splendid progress."

"I am," I said. "You look lovely. How are the children?"

"Wonderful," she replied. "They are so happy to know that you're much better, and they can't wait until they can come to visit you. They'll come to see you before long. They sent you some pictures they have drawn for you, and they wrote some messages for you as keepsakes."

Overjoyed, I examined their pictures and pocketed their writings to read later. Mary said: "All three children are happy and in fine health. They are doing very well in school, and love it. Kenneth is changing fast. He's growing, and is getting to be a real boy in every way now. Fred, you'll never be able to tease him for being a little sissy again, or call him his mother's little boy. He asks about you all the time, and he acts more like you every day. He loves his kindergarten, and the girls like their school life and piano lessons." She went on: "Do you need anything? Can I help you in any way, Fred?"

"Yes," I replied. "Can you arrange for me to wear some regular street trousers? Getting away from these overalls would be a big help! Also, I want my low-top shoes so that I won't have to wear these heavy clodhoppers. I want to dress as I'm used to doing. And I need my wrist watch; I hate to have to bother others about the time."

Mary agreed. "Of course. I'll talk with the staff about these matters." Before the short visit ended, she said, "I'll see you again this week, and I shall visit you often." As she departed, we both were smiling and happy. I was proud of her, and her visit gave me more confidence and self-respect.

My patient-friends were glad for me. They greeted my return with such comments as: "Boy, but your wife is beautiful! She looks and acts like a real lady." One said, "She looks like an angel." Another remarked, "Why, Doc, she acts like she really does care about you and believe in you." Others eagerly asked, "When is she coming again? Can we meet her next time? Won't you bring her in to see us?"

As a result of Mary's visit, I was given a pair of my own trousers, a belt, a shirt, and my wrist watch. These items gave my morale a real lift.

That night I wrote our three children a postal card headed with my slogan "AT HOME MORE AND MORE EACH MONTH IN 1954!" I added, "I had a great visit from your sweet Mommy today. She brought lots of nice things and love from the whole family. The writing materials, stamps, pen, and wonderful little messages from you three children will help Daddy more than you will ever know. Thanks for the letters, pictures, and keepsakes she brought from you!"

The next day, while writing to Mary to thank her for a surprise letter and also for the kindnesses of our church friends, I included one of the few reports of my growing faith. In a restrained and guarded manner, I wrote: "I, too, believe that beyond our human ability, or even need to understand, God is dealing some unusual cards of love and care that He will not let go wasted."

In another letter, on the second day after her first visit, I wrote Mary: "With my mind as clear as it now is, I have the firm faith and conviction that complete recovery will come here, and that it is mainly a matter of time." Meanwhile, I mentioned "a grand talk with Dr. Shultz" (the director of our ward at that time) "this morning at my request." I noted that the "patients in this Male Insulin Department seem to think highly of Doctors Estes, Buffaloe, and Young above all, and many of them like Shultz. (About all of them highly like the chaplain.)"

I included a note for our children:

How are you three tots doing? Your love is so grand and good to have. Your daddy thinks of you often. And he feels you are so sweet to let Mommy come and help your daddy some. Soon, maybe we'll be having some family picnics! How about that? I'll send some messages by Mommy on Thursday when she will visit me the second time.

They give us plenty to eat here each day. Daddy drinks extra milk until he almost pops. . . . Thanks for the things—grand things—you sent through Mommy.

Love,
DADDY

Some of the patients were hurt and bitter because their closest friends and relatives did not so much as write to them, much less visit them. They begged me to read my letters from my wife, relatives, and friends. I did this often.

On Thursday, February 4th, I could hardly wait for Mary's visit. Just before she arrived, I gratefully wrote to my father:

DEAR DAD,

Yours of February 3 does me a lot of good. To me, it is a great and helpful letter, giving the boost and encouragement of the types that only a deeply respected father can give to his youngest child and son. May God bless you and our whole family, and our life together for it.

I'm recovering fast. I feel fine and almost fully like my old self. When I do fully recover, I trust that your letter, which arrived this morning, will hit a lot of nails on the head for the future. Right now, we'll just wait and cross all the bridges as they come. I am learning something from a side of life that is fascinating and worth while. The chances are that what you say about "too much work and lack of sleep" will come as close as anything to getting at the fundamental cause of this breakdown, no matter what terms are used.

Your reports of the churches are most encouraging. Also, I am glad to get the news about the garden plans. Please follow through on the manure plans for Mother's flowers. I hope to see both of you before too many weeks or months.

53

I've had cards and letters from almost all over the country. It is most helpful to see that so many friends do not forget one who has gotten out of action. Among so many things, I was thrilled lately with a great word from Gretna [the Christian Church at Gretna, Virginia, which I had served as a student pastor during three of my Lynchburg College years]. All the names were as clear as a bell. . . .

Hope you are well. I'm looking forward today to the second visit from Mary.

Love,
FRED

When Mary came, I explained what it would mean to some of the patients to meet her and for her to give them individual attention. I said, "Besides, I want you to know my new friends and ward companions." She gladly met them. The patients were enthusiastic about her visit. After Mary left, I shared the candy, cookies, and cigarettes which she had brought me. All these gifts disappeared in a few minutes, and the taste of genuine home cooking seemed to boost the spirit of our ward life. In addition, manufactured cigarettes delighted some patients, who had been rolling their own from such hospital smoking rations as they could get.

That night I wrote to my brother, Dr. William G. West, the minister of the First Christian Church, Chattanooga, Tennessee. My emerging attitude and hopes were apparent:

DEAR BILL,

I still feel great. For a solid week, my tired mind and spirit have felt clear as a bell. Of course, during the 5:00–10:00 A.M. insulin shock treatments of real magnitude, we all go through convulsions, comas and dizziness normally. This regular series is from Monday through Friday. Saturdays and Sundays are more free and with less rugged schedules.

Mary came by Monday and today in the afternoons. Her personal visits have been "out of this world" in every way. What a solid wife and lover she has been and has remained! She is beginning to bring batches of letters and cards, which I can read and handle easily now. They mean a lot at this stage in the game of insulin treatments and recovery. They come almost literally from all over the nation. Our church has risen to heights of loyalty, love, and understanding.

I am cooperating in every way I can. I have complete faith in full and complete recovery, with the best years ahead of these rest months.

Thanks for all the great help and understanding, especially during the days that I shall perhaps not remember or recall until the treatments are completed. But you and George have been the great brothers, always appreciated, long before this acid test.

I've had two long reading periods in the Medical Dictionary. In many ways, it would be most helpful to see you and George within a few weeks. But we'll cross the bridges when they come. For God's sake, get your rest amply now before it ever seems needed. FRED

During my months at State Hospital, I was helped immensely by Mary's frequent visits. She was often allowed to take me to a nearby private home of a friend on the hospital grounds. The private, informal atmosphere of a regular house and yard was refreshing, a true change from the drab hospital ward and building nearby. It was at this house that I met Dr. Walter Sikes, whom I liked immensely. I knew from the grapevine that he was to become the new superintendent of State Hospital on July 1, 1954. Except for the chaplain, he was the only specialist at Dix Hill who called me "Fred."

Mary helped to fill in the gaps in my loss of memory involving the period prior to my breakdown. I was not worried about the loss of memory, but very curious. I kept wondering why so many letters from friends mentioned my overwork and heavy schedule before my crack-up. I let her know that I already knew about my electric shock treatments at Graylyn from the Hill's grapevine.

She said: "Among your normal duties as the minister of our Raleigh church, you continued to teach nine semester hours a week at Atlantic Christian College in Wilson, North Carolina, through June of 1953. You were doing this ever since we moved to Raleigh about three years before." In addition, Mary told me: "You were on the commission to draft a 'Restatement of the Position of the Christian Churches for the Twentieth Century' which was adopted by the 1953 International Convention of the Disciples of Christ at Portland, Oregon. In fact, you wrote the final wording of the draft as submitted and recommended by your committee for convention action."

"I did?" I asked. "I don't remember doing so."

"Also," she said, "you took a month's trip to the convention with me and some other members of our church by way of California, the Grand Canyon, Yellowstone National Park, and other places of interest."

"I did?" I replied. "It's all a blank to me."

She smiled. "That was in July. In November, you presided over the state convention of the Disciples of Christ of North Carolina at Winston-Salem. I can see you don't remember that either; it was only the week before you broke down. You don't recall it now, Fred, but you were the president of the state convention last year. And in the spring you held a preaching mission for Sam Freeman's church in East Orange, New Jersey. And you took two long trips to Missouri: one for a series of lectures at our state ministers' retreat at Culver-Stockton College, and another for a preaching mission in Kansas City. Why are you so amused, Fred? You also gave addresses at several colleges and universities. On the side, you served as president of the Raleigh Tennis Association, president of the Eastern

Carolina Tennis Association, and vice president of the Raleigh Ministerial Association. And that's not all."

At my request Mary prepared a list of my major engagements for 1953. She brought them to me on one of her early visits. The jammed schedule of extra speaking engagements afforded me laughs at myself for weeks to come. However, when she later brought me copies of the "Restatement of the Position of the Disciples of Christ" and of my speech at the Portland convention in behalf of the Board of Higher Education for our communion, I did not laugh. Immediately, I recalled the pages word for word. Delighted, I noted: "I have not really forgot my writings and addresses prior to November, 1953. But I have lost my memory of such events, dates, and places. Dimly these experiences seem familiar, but not vivid and personal. The details are missing. Maybe they'll fill in later."

Soon the children were allowed, at intervals, to come with my wife to visit me. The high spots in these meetings came when we had private family picnics on the hospital grounds on several Saturday afternoons. We often cooked hot dogs together, and sometimes steaks, over an open fireplace. The hugs, laughter, and enthusiasm of our three children boosted my spirits and helped me to forget the grinding impact of the deep shock treatments. I marveled at the way the children were growing. George Kenneth was five years of age, Rebecca Lynn seven, and Mary Margaret ten.

Usually Mary came to see me with some fascinating story about the children's experiences. One day, she had been driving alone with little Kenneth in the car and had accidentally run past a stop light. She said, "I looked around cautiously and didn't see another soul. I told Kenneth: 'My, but we were lucky! There are no police to see us and give us a ticket. And nobody to report us for missing a red light."

"Kenneth replied, 'Yeah! And God can't talk, can He, Mommy?' '

A few week-end visits at our parsonage with my wife and children were granted. These trips home were full of joy and challenge. The girls played the piano for me, and all three children sang songs.

Upon each visit, to and from the hospital, I was startled by the sign posted at the entrance gates of Dix Hill. It pierced me when I saw:

H 7
DIX HILL
State Hospital for Insane
Authorized 1849, largely
through efforts of Dorothea L. Dix.
500 yards Southwest

I observed: " 'State Hospital for Insane' indeed! This is an honest monument to the past history of Dix Hill when it was no genuine hospital at all, except in name, but only a legal prison in which to confine the mentally ill. It has not been too long since they first employed a few registered nurses, not to mention psychiatrists. The old prison traditions still linger. I am a patient at the time when both the old and the new heritages are at war behind the scenes. Thank God there are other signs that this place is on the way toward becoming a real hospital—to help patients get well! But it has yet a long way to go. It can't improve much faster without a more informed public with a conscience and understanding about us patients and about staff needs. This ignorant, prejudiced sign is posted by North Carolina's Historical Society!"

The sign was blown down by Hurricane Hazel in October, 1954. So far, it has not been replaced, to the delight of patients and the less *status quo* types on the staff.

When other relatives came from a long distance to see me, I silently wondered, "What do they think when they see that sign at the gates?" Nevertheless, when my mother visited me it was thrilling to see her again. Mary's father and mother, Mr. and Mrs. Guy H. Lewis, came down several times from Lynchburg, Virginia. And my brothers, George and Bill, came together from Tennessee and spent several days with Mary and the children. This gave us time for lengthy talks, but the subject of the sign never came up. To know at firsthand that my family and in-laws understood me and were pulling for my recovery and return to normal life was a lift that only could have come from their personal visits.

Increasingly I pondered the inspiration of my family to me. In doing this, I often recalled how the cowboy in Owen Wister's novel *The Virginian* had wasted his own life and talents, only to be driven to a nobler and richer life. I appreciated anew his explanation of his changed life, as he tried to say, "It was nobody's preaching or praying that made a better man of me—but two or three people believing in me and thinking and expecting more highly of me than I deserved— and I felt like I just could not let them down!"

I noted that letters from my relatives and friends always shared growing faith in my progress, final recovery, and return to society. Frequently they stressed that "your best years are ahead." They wrote such messages of cheer, hope, confidence, and prayer so often that I was convinced, "They really do believe in me and are not merely trying to say nice things to make me feel better."

Yet, increasingly, I observed the hurt faces of some patients when mail came for almost every person but them. Their sadness, disappointment, and bitter claims were expressed by one who said, "We have no wife, sweetheart, relative, or friend who cares a damn where we are or what will happen to us." They did not feel that they "belonged" to anybody or to any cause other than that of their own lonely roles. To them, confinement to what they called "this insane asylum" was like the kiss of doom.

I thought, "How odd it is that some patients receive money when all they want is a touch of home—some homemade gifts or home-sent letters of love and remembrance, and especially a visit from some member of their families!"

Starving for news from loved ones, patients crowded around me when I opened my own mail. They vicariously felt that it was "their" news from "home" too. They rejoiced with me, and were happier for a while in spite of their own neglected plights. They eagerly asked if my wife, brothers, or parents had "good news." I often reread for them portions of letters, and they seemed to feel better. My folks and friends knew just what to write for my condition, which was also the condition of most of my fellow patients.

The touch of my home and family helped me to feel more at home in our ward. And these contacts by mail and personal visits helped to make the ward a more healthy family of friends who cared and shared with one another. To accept, and to be accepted by, one's own family was a healthy experience.

6

Our Ward-Life Fraternity

Feeling at home with my family again while I was a patient was one thing. There were old ties and familiar landmarks to guide me. However, to accept fully the new status and traditions of ward life was quite a different test.

Soon I got intimately acquainted with my fellow patients. For a few fleeting weeks I was amused and fascinated by their conversations, insulin "shop talks," and debates. Their efforts to tease and play pranks took on increasing meaning as time went on, involving a rigid schedule of deadly monotony and tension over shock treatments. Almost anything to break the routine was a relief.

The patients could always resort to their two favorite topics of discussion: sex and religion, in that order. "At least," I thought, "my comrades surpass what is regarded as normal and natural in the outside world. They do not have to talk about the weather in order to make conversation. But they are not superior to normal society in originality in handling their pet subjects." Every few days they exhausted their knowledge, jokes, and theories about sex and religion.

This indoor sport did not daunt or bore them. A steady turnover of new patients, replacing the outgoing patients who had finished their comas, gave them a fresh audience to repeat the same old script and performances. While initiating our incoming patients into our Royster Building community, they could expound their ideas of sex and religion incessantly. The subjects did not change; the audiences did.

Noting their crude notions of sex and religion, I stayed out of their serious discussions on both subjects. I asked myself, "In spite of heated arguments and superstitions in these matters, why is it that their dogmatic disagreements never break their friendships? No one ever changes anyone else's point of view. They seem to enjoy these seesawing debates and repetitions just as long as they are free to expound and exchange their individual opinions. I wonder why they preach and make long speeches on issues which are more theoretical than practical to them. Rarely is anything said which has to do with their own personal lives."

This gave me food for private thought. Often I puzzled: "What is the real difference between this little hospital fraternity and most college and university faculties, and even churches? That is, except for less education, sophistication, and class snobbery. What difference do these monologues and arguments make in anyone's life or sense of values?"

Sometimes I was asked to referee or judge between conflicting opinions when they were deadlocked. This I refused to do. But occasionally I enjoyed the fun of raising teasing little questions to upset their routine of discussing the same old things. Then I would slip off to the ward's office to read, leaving the patients in loud arguments. A nurse caught on to this role. Chuckling, she asked, "Dr. West, why do you pull such pranks? You do it just for plain devilment, don't you? That's like taking candy from babies. But I admit it's funny to watch you leave them arguing among themselves!"

However, in one religious area they did agree spontaneously. Although they never seemed to resent my refusal to share my own faith and religious convictions, they usually begged me to pray for them. When bedtime was called every night, some patient would plead: "Dr. West, will you remember me tonight in your prayers? Please ask God not to let me die during tomorrow's shock treatment." As the weeks passed, I usually visited each cooperative patient before retiring at night, assuring him that he would do fine and get well. And I would pat the withdrawn patients on their shoulders silently. When I went to bed, I did pray privately for each patient every night. But I always refused to pray out loud for the whole ward in spite of many such requests.

I kept asking myself: "Why do these fellows seem to respect me religiously? Why do they ask me especially to pray for them and to mention them by name before God? Most of them share a low opinion of clergymen in general. Not many of them have ever met a minister like me before. Few of them are connected actively with any churches. Mostly they come from cult types of churches rather than from the main-stream movements of Christendom. Except for their common interest in prayer and their fear of death, their religious views seem to make little difference in how life is really lived and faced. I wonder why."

Finally I asked: "Why do you ask me to pray for you? I know how you feel about preachers. But I don't even talk about my beliefs with you. From what some of you say about religion, it seems to me that I would appear irreligious or nonreligious to you."

One spokesman replied: "We often talk about these things—when you're not around. At first I thought you were the most irreligious preacher I ever saw. Others did too. Because you don't go around quoting the Bible, offering to pray for us, and getting after us about our cussing, dirty jokes, and hard talk against preachers and churches. Nothing we say gets you riled up. But, Dr. West, I been thinking for a long time now you are real religious down deep inside. But you don't brag about it or try to put on a big sideshow about what you believe and how you pray. Most of these other guys feel the same way about you too.

"You're a praying man. None of us has heard you cuss and yell when you come out of a shock treatment. You don't beg for your mother or daddy like some do. All you ever say is, 'O God!' or maybe, 'God help me!' Yes, sir, you're religious in our book, but you got it where it really counts. Most of us just talk about religion. But when we face those shock treatments and are scared to die without the Lord's help, we all pray. The difference is, we don't know how to pray right. We haven't been learned yet. Some of us figure that your prayers count more than ours."

I was moved and dumfounded. But other patients insisted that our friend was right. From then on, I avoided such questions and conversations.

Nevertheless, as time passed, I was bored at hearing the same old subjects, but I always liked the patients themselves. Chats with staff members relieved me greatly, no matter what their interests were. And I wanted to learn more about insulin treatments and their various theories. I spent many hours each week studying the Medical Dictionary in the office, especially in regard to mental and emotional illnesses. And I read all the material about their treatments which I could get smuggled through the grapevine.

Dr. E. H. Schultz, the first director of our ward, was wonderful to me. We had mutual friends in the outside world and interests in sports. He came from a profoundly religious background. In time, Dr. Frank Badrock replaced Dr. Schultz to direct the ward. The former was a friendly Englishman from South Africa. Staff and patients respected and liked him. His subtle dry wit and humor were like a tonic to our spirits. He was unusually kind and understanding. Patients looked forward to his arrival as they did to Chaplain Steininger's frequent visits.

Boredom grew into restlessness for me. The constant chatter about sex and religion ceased to be curious and novel. When my restlessness was at its peak, Dr. Badrock informed me: "Soon we shall be receiving an incoming patient in this ward. He'll be choice company for you. He's a young businessman of good educational background; he has a variety of interests that will mean a lot to you. You and he should hit it off well together."

When the patient arrived, he was assigned to the bed next to mine in the front corner of our ward. As he approached, it was obvious that he was not the quiet, shy type. He acted as though he were an old friend of the attendants and nurses whom he had just met. Obviously he was a lovable fellow. Introducing himself, he announced, "My name is B. O. Slaughter. Wouldn't those initials just kill you?"

At first, we thought he was kidding. But when I glanced at his name on the card placed on his bed, I knew that he had a rare sense of humor. Chuckling, he explained, "You fellows can just call me 'B.O.,' but it may be hard to get me out of this ward!"

However, we were amused at how seriously Slaughter accepted some higher staff members' promises that insulin shock treatments are "not painful or anything to worry about; they're nothing more than going to sleep; you'll never know you had them." We were used to such approaches to incoming patients and their families, and often wished that the doctors had a few comas themselves before describing them so glibly to others. These evasions of truth increased tensions between some patients and their innocent relatives, who assumed that mental patients are too sick to get such facts straight.

During his first night with us, B. O. learned why some staff members were hated. Our ward leader, John, kept us awake for hours, screaming in pain. Finally we coaxed an attendant to call a doctor. A cocky young foreign doctor came, looking us over with scorn and disgust. "Meester, what ees the trouble with yuh?" he asked.

John replied, "My god-damn' ankle is about to kill me. I can't stand the pains no more."

The doctor jeered: "Yuh don't have pains—jeest psychosomatic complaints to get yourself some attention. Meester, yuh jeest theenk yuh have pains!" Then he paraded out, leaving John in agony. In-

65

dignant that John received no examination, some patients wanted to kill the doctor. I thought an attendant might actually punch the doctor in the nose before he got out.

During his second day B. O., with the rest of us, watched a fellow patient die under insulin treatment. Afterward, a nurse and doctor explained to us: "Mr. —— did not die under shock treatment. He had already had his glucose and orange juice, and was fully recovered. He died from a heart attack." These explanations were repeated too often while other staff members remained silent, red-faced, and embarrassed. For the first time we heard that "taking a hot shower is no part of shock treatments." For the umpteenth time we were assured, "We have never lost a patient yet during insulin shock treatment in the male ward."

That night we were still badly shaken, knowing that the victim could have been any of us. Cursing the staff and hospital, some patients came to me. A spokesman said: "Doc, we heard that poor guy tell you last night that his heart was about to kill him. We heard you beg them to examine him. You know they made fun of him—just like they did John. This guy wasn't in no shape to take these damn' treatments. We all been saying that ever since he came. They killed him, the bastards! They been telling us, all the time, that we had to take the hot showers to complete every treatment. Ain't that right? We saw them choke him up with orange juice. He died before he could ever sit up, much less take a shower."

I replied: "Yes, you're right. But that's the way they keep their records here. They tell us and the public that they've never yet lost a male insulin patient from a treatment. Maybe this is why their record is perfect, beating the nation's 2 per cent or so fatality average. We can't fight them now, but when we get out we can help improve this whole situation. Don't be too hard on the hospital. The day will come, before we get too old, when such lying and blunders will not go on. They don't have enough staff yet, and medical ethics and standards stink here now. The whole grapevine knows how they keep their records. In a sense they are telling the truth, for everyone dies from a heart attack; his heart has to stop beating."

The tension was terrific. Suddenly, John broke it by explaining, "Meester, yuh ain't daid; yuh jeest theenk yuh ees daid!" We all laughed. Perhaps this humor saved some staff member's life. But it did not save the life of a later incoming patient whom we loved and respected. The grapevine reported his death to me in the fall, soon after he began his second series of insulin treatments.

B. O. became a good canasta player. Within a few days, he and I had taught several of the progressive patients how to play the game, which was new to them. This was a welcome change from gin rummy. Whenever possible, some attendants joined us. B. O. and I became close friends and constant companions. From the moment of his colorful arrival, the patients and staff tended to congregate in our front corner of the ward. B. O.'s hearty laugh was contagious. His record player and choice of classical and popular music meant much to me. He loved to sing. He had been a leader of congregational church singing, and was an informed churchman. But he was entirely uninhibited in singing any songs, sacred or profane. Soon we had developed our own ward version of "The Battle Hymn of the Republic." When B. O. and I would recover enough from our shock treatments to stagger together toward the showers, we would lock arms and march, singing the regular first verse and shouting the chorus, "Glory, glory, hallelujah! His truth is marching on." Then we would stamp our feet as loudly as possible and scream to the rhythm, "Tramp! Tramp! Tramp!" The staff often watched in tolerant amusement, while the patients laughed gleefully.

However, this new variety of ward life did not ease my growing concern about the purpose and need of "sixty comas" to complete our insulin course. The part of the treatments which I loathed the most was when I was revived to consciousness. Seldom could I identify my own hands and feet as belonging to my body. I felt completely disintegrated, literally all to pieces. Seconds and minutes

seemed like centuries while I desperately struggled to restore my
identity. Being strapped to the bed when I craved to get up was
equally frustrating. Most of the times my memory was erased, and
my mind blurred as far as rational thought was involved. When this
happened, I was frightened and helpless beyond description. In
addition my thirst was insatiable even after drinking the usual three
glasses of sugary, canned orange juice. These experiences were more
trying than my former nightmares.

Eventually, I became obsessed with the fear that I might not recover from one of the treatments. I did not fear death; I had accepted
the Lord as my Shepherd. But I was afraid that after some treatment
I might only "come to" just enough for my mind to remain perma-
nently confused, fragmented, or irrational. I was anxious to retain
what "clearing up" and degree of recovery had already been achieved.
Also, I was puzzled as to why the staff had not voluntarily told
me what diagnosis had been made by the staff meeting for that purpose. And it did not make sense to me that the staff would not allow
us patients to lie down in bed and rest or sleep after exhausting treatments. I could hardly keep my eyes open when I fought tiredness
and drowsiness for hours every afternoon. (This policy was out of
line with the rest recommended for insulin shock patients, just as
for T.B. patients, by experts.)

I had gathered all the information I could about the various
schools of insulin theory and treatments. As I considered the varie-
ties of approach, I debated with myself: "Why are sixty comas necessary at State Hospital for insulin shock patients? Why not thirty or
one hundred? At one hospital they administer light shocks, not giving sufficient insulin to burn up enough of the body's sugar content
to allow a patient to reach the coma level. At another hospital, they
do give deep insulin shock treatments, but they vary the number
required for individual patients according to the needs and responses
of the persons involved. I favor the latter practice myself, for they
combine personal work by psychiatrists with the shock treatments

to determine the patient's possible needs for further insulin therapy. I question State Hospital's extreme theory and practice of requiring sixty comas for every insulin ward patient, regardless of the progress or condition of any individual. This may be all right for hogs on a mass basis, but why for *people?* Why this impersonal nonhuman approach without any use of psychiatry directly with the human patient?"

When I could no longer repress these tensions, I shared the problems with my wife. I asked: "Mary, how about your arranging an appointment for me with the psychiatrist who presided over the staff meeting when I was interviewed as Exhibit A for a diagnosis? I knew him personally long before I became a patient here. As far as I know, he had long been the top psychiatrist at Dix Hill. I respect him highly. He's a likable fellow, and ought to be able to put the cards on the table with real authority. I haven't even seen him privately since I've been in the insulin ward. This has been a big disappointment. At least, I think I deserve to know at firsthand what their official diagnosis is. I cannot understand this hospital's 100 per cent physical or organic approach to mentally ill patients. Since I've been in this ward, I've talked with a psychiatrist just twice—and only for a few moments. He discussed mainly his own problems—not mine—about lack of adequate staff and suitable working conditions for his own role. He's a nice guy. But I think I'm ready now for some personal psychiatric help and guidance. Or else I want to be transferred from here to a hospital where I can get individual attention from a psychiatrist."

Mary replied: "All right, Fred. I think that's the best thing to try to do. I'll do my best to get you the appointment. You've been so concerned about these problems that I think some qualified specialist should help you to understand the situation soon."

The conference was arranged. By then I had already received credit for thirty official comas. I knew that most patients averaged over eighty deep shock treatments before receiving credit for sixty comas. Staff members had explained that the Dix Hill view of a coma was when "a patient does not respond in any physical way to any outside stimulus such as the striking of a joint, or, better, when an outsider can lift one's eyelid and touch one's eyeball without any blinking or motion from the patient." This, too, had me puzzled, for it was not implied in any definition or description of a coma in the out-of-date medical dictionary I found in the office.

The psychiatrist gave me plenty of time, answering all my questions. He was quite dignified and formal in his approach, as though he had never known me before I became a patient. Most of his discourse sounded as if he were reciting old classroom lectures.

I popped my first question: "Doctor, I'm interested in the outcome of the staff meeting for my diagnosis. What was the official diagnosis, if you don't mind telling me as a patient?"

"Schizophrenia with paranoid tendencies," he replied.

This was no surprise. I had expected it, but was relieved to hear it said authoritatively. However, as I vaguely recalled my condition before the clearing-up stages, I had wondered if I did not also have some symptoms of manic depressiveness—and if it were not possible to have a variety of major types of mental illnesses all at the same time, as one could with physical illnesses. But this was mainly a matter of theory to me; I was not bothered, but only curious about this interest. Therefore I did not pursue the subject.

I asked: "How about the theory and practice of sixty comas before any patient can complete the course of insulin shock treatments here? Why not more or less? Why this particular number? It seems to me that there are as many schools of thought in this realm as there are in Biblical criticism."

The psychiatrist replied: "Dr. West, this is our practice here at State Hospital. We don't know exactly why sixty is the optimum or magic number. But we have found from our experience that sixty comas do bring the best results in the long run. Not every patient may need sixty, but we treat them all alike. We find that when patients have sixty comas, the chances are less for possible relapses later on and for readmissions to the hospital. There are a variety of approaches in insulin therapy, but we specialize here in this number."

He assured me that I ought to take the sixty comas as "a matter of insurance" against the possible return of the illness. He kindly, but firmly, let me know that I had no other option and that I would be wise to reconcile myself to this schedule. At the same time, he commended me for my rapid improvement, cooperation, and behavior as a patient. "But," he said, "I want to apologize for our keeping you locked up with the other patients in your ward. We are not used to having many patients in your category, with your background. I hope you'll understand why we must apply these rules to all our patients alike."

I thought to myself: "If that's all you know of my individual case, I'll keep quiet on the subject. I haven't resented the idea of being locked in ever since I cleared up." Yet I was surprised that a psychiatrist of his status should try to comfort me as the nurses and attendants did, at a time when I had no problem at all.

Before our lengthy session ended, I raised a question as innocently as possible: "Have the psychological tests which I was given been of any real aid? For example, sir, did they help toward my official diagnosis at the staff meeting with me?"

"Oh, yes, indeed," he replied. "These psychological tests were invaluable in making your diagnosis. We use the results for every patient before the staff makes a diagnosis."

After that we talked about other matters. But I wondered why they collected such scientific data at all in State Hospital. If what the doctor had said was true, why were my psychological tests not given until many days after the staff had met with me and had already made the official diagnosis? But I knew that I had better be mum in that regard if I ever wanted to get out of the hospital and be accepted as sane again. And I knew that I'd better not hint at what

71

I had learned over the grapevine, for it only confirmed the gossip. This encounter gave me confidence in myself and in my recovery. Now I was sure that I was fully rational again, and that I was already as objective, or more so, in the pursuit of truth and in facing reality than was this popular, recognized psychiatrist. Also I felt that I, not trained as a scientist, was more interested in scientific truth for its own sake than this "scientist" was either for my sake or for that of science. I concluded, "Maybe they are being good politicians and promoters by reporting routine psychological tests on their books and records in order to appear more scientific and up to date than they really are." In any case, I knew that this was the hospital's and public's problem, not mine. I resolved to finish my quota of sixty comas without protest or further questions.

Other events helped to break our weekly grind of inevitable insulin treatment. Once each week we attended a movie together. Every Sunday morning those who wished attended chapel. The chapel sessions meant a great deal to most other patients as well as to me. The chaplain led a sound worship service for all levels and backgrounds. His messages were profoundly religious, yet simple and practical. They were full of hope and understanding, speaking to our conditions as patients and staff combined.

An increasing number of outdoor picnics and hikes were tonic for our whole ward. Such group activities, together with throwing a football and some mild outdoor games, were great reliefs from the dull building and typical ward life inside. They broke the routine of marching downstairs like prisoners to get our trays at a foul-smelling kitchen and carrying our trays back up the flights of steps to our ward, only to return them later in the same puppetlike fashion. Music and group singing added to the variety of interests, but not until B. O. had arrived. Hearing radio broadcasts of North Carolina State College basketball games and big-league baseball contests helped too, but few of the other patients had such interests. I usually "broke the rules" and heard the games with the staff in areas forbidden to patients in general, enjoying the extra "bootlegged" coffee while I was there.

Our ward had two extremely colorful characters who stole the show and our hearts. We enjoyed these self-appointed saviors of mankind. Whenever possible, we enticed them to elaborate on their special missions to save mankind in their own unique roles, especially when visitors and officials were in our room.

A stocky little man who called himself "The Tallest Tree on Earth" and "The Furtherest Kid on Earth" had his own specialized vocabulary that had meaning for him only. He did not need to be coaxed to talk. Often his excited monologues burst forth spontaneously. When recovering from treatments, he gave indignant orations about the "way they think they can treat the Tallest Tree and the Furtherest Kid."

He reviewed his history: "That ignorant sheriff didn't have sense enough to know who the Tallest Tree on Earth is. No, he didn't even know who the Furtherest Kid on Earth was after he had already seen me. The sheriff was crazy. He was crazy because he took me and put handcuffs on me and had me locked up in this damn' crazy insane asylum. The sheriff hisself should of been put in this asylum, not the Tallest Tree. That proves he was crazy. All these doctors and nurses are crazy too, or they wouldn't keep me locked up here. The idea of taking me from my tobacco farm, where I was happy! They're all crazy—just plain nuts. I ain't going to stay here."

If anybody challenged the Tallest Tree and the Furtherest Kid's pet words and title, he exploded with anger. Under such tension, he begged me to help "identify" him, since "the Bible tells all about me as the Tallest Tree and the Furtherest Kid." Sympathetically, I gave my assurance: "There never was anybody else like you. I know that."

Our other unique character was the "Eight-Star General," as he styled himself. He, too, had a special means of identification, for he was the general who ruled the secret "South Planet." We patients never tired of hearing the monologues and speeches of the Tallest Tree and the Eight-Star General. We enjoyed them, and they enjoyed our audience. Few of the staff were as patient, refusing to listen to their special claims. But we wouldn't have robbed them of their special missions in history or in our ward for anything.

Although it was a "top military secret" which he would not reveal even to us, the Eight-Star General claimed: "I really won the last world war with a secret mission of my troops from the South Planet. In fact, you can ask General Eisenhower and other famous American generals—if they are free to tell the truth. I gave them private advice they needed several times to win crucial battles and to plan the big secret strategy that won out."

The Eight-Star General not only was the ruler of the mysterious South Planet; he also had made history on earth. "I was the greatest big-league baseball pitcher in history," he modestly confided. (He was a smiling, shy type, who always spoke quietly, never yelling or raising his voice as the Furtherest Kid did.) He said, "Of course, this isn't in the record books. The big managers agreed to keep it quiet because they didn't want to embarrass their regular stars like Babe Ruth and the others."

For demonstrations of his pitching skills, which he always volunteered to give, I was drafted as his make-believe catcher. He would tolerate no other. He claimed: "You are the only one who understands the secret signals and my tricky wind-ups. My surprise deliveries might injure some of you guys. But Doc, he can handle most of my stuff behind the plate." The other patients usually lined up and cheered him, while I coaxed him to throw me his "up-shoot-drop curves" and his "fast slow balls." I also umpired. He would beam with delight when I would smack my imaginary mitt and yell, "Strike!"

One day, long before his baseball talents came to light, I had won the General's grateful friendship. He had confided to the ward how many times he had "swum the English Channel—even when I had to break the ice to do it." The patients accepted that modest boast. But when he insisted that he was the "first person ever to swim the Atlantic Ocean without stops or rests," that was too much for his other ward mates. They howled with laughter, calling for "proof." His feelings deeply hurt, he looked to me for support.

I said: "Yes, boys, the General is right! I know that he did swim the Atlantic Ocean and was the first person to do it. I saw him do it myself. I was only a few yards behind him all the way, and he beat me fairly and squarely. I was the second person ever to swim the Atlantic Ocean." We all laughed. Even the General grinned, but he was happy.

The self-appointed ruler of the South Planet was tall, lanky, and awkward for a great athlete. But in any case he was the ablest checker player—the most clever general and tactician—I ever saw. When anybody doubted his rule over the South Planet, the General invited him for a "personal duel at the checker board to prove it." He won such battles when he had his choice of weapons.

After B. O. joined us, we organized pranks at the expense of student nurses. Their tenure with us lasted only a week apiece. Their turnover was rapid enough for our tricks not to grow stale. Most student nurses were too young, optimistic, and trusting to be case-hardened. They had not yet acquired the conventional guarded and detached approach of patient-wise registered nurses. They could not disguise their own personal shock at faked convulsions or at first seeing patients react with hoax animalism as though relapsing in comas. B. O. and I would fake "passing out" when the naïve new student nurses came on duty with our ward. Other patients would show alarm and send the frightened nurses rushing to our aid. When greeted with laughter, they were good little sports. We loved them and they did us good. They neither bore personal grudges nor offered professional excuses for their own limitations and inexperience.

We organized a human barnyard, breaking the dreaded routine of our early-morning schedules on treatment days. As new student nurses appeared, we pretended to sleep and snore. Suddenly one patient would crow like a rooster; another would moo like a cow. Being mostly farmers, the entire group could excel at that game. Dogs barked, crows cawed, pigs squealed, cats fought or made love, and pigeons cooed. Rural life was dramatized.

We gradually learned that ward life does not have to be dull or uninteresting, for patients can be creative. The sooner the most pathetic patients took part in our community life, the more quickly they were on the highroad to recovery.

7

Entering the Outside World Again

Before my dismissal as a patient, my contacts with the outside world multiplied. The more I understood myself and our ward life, the less uneasy I was at facing normal society again.

Reading helped greatly. At first only the sports pages could renew my vivid interest in daily newspapers. I reflected: "Front-page news stories discourage me. They are not for my own good yet, for I tend to identify myself too much with tragic personalities and events. For my own sake, I've got to learn to sift the chaff from the wheat in all reading. Any tendency toward personal distress, self-pity, and tragedy as a result of reading should warn me that my old hostile island may again loom on my horizon. Especially is this true now. But I can read sports without identifying myself either with the victims or with the victors of human struggle and conflicts. Already I am objective enough about sports and their various heroes and scapegoats. This is real progress. But I mustn't bite off more reading variety than I can digest, for the sake of my own health."

Mary brought all sorts of popular magazines and novels. The other patients gleefully borrowed the slick picture magazines, which challenged them almost as much as their comic books. Daily I thrived upon the cartoons about "Dennis the Menace." In particular, I appreciated the *Reader's Digest* condensed novels, and any articles about new phases of life and interest in the outside world.

Personal letters from former students, professors, and religious leaders throughout the nation meant more and more to me as my confinement neared its end. I felt: "It's inspiring to realize that so many concerned friends are remembering me in their thoughts and prayers. I am not alone in my struggle to make a comeback. Beyond this hill, people whom I love and respect are hopeful, believing in the ultimate outcome of faith and effort. The public will be more friendly, understanding, and helpful than I had expected."

Nevertheless, the gnawing dread of facing normal society again was too deep for words. I kept deciding: "I'll have to let this problem work itself out when I actually am ready to face it. My immediate job now is to do the best I can where I am." Yet I kept asking myself: "What will the average citizen think of me? Will my hospitalization be held against me? Or will the average citizen give me a fair trial to prove myself? I hope that people will judge my new health and life on their own merits!"

One letter stood out above all to help me adjust to this tension. It was from Dr. Kenneth Scott Latourette, my major professor at the Yale Divinity School. To know that I was on this great man's daily prayer list strengthened my faith. I had long admired his personal Christian faith and devotional life, as well as scholarship. I regarded him as the world's leading Protestant "monk," however unofficial the title. A bachelor, wedded to the Church, his books are his children shared among all who study the history of the spread of Christianity throughout the world.

Professor Latourette wrote often, describing his own personal hopes for me, and his Christian convictions and prayers. One letter, particularly, probed the depths of my anxiety about the future. He told me how, as a young man, his own health and career had been interrupted. Because of a critical eye disease, Latourette had been forced to leave China as a missionary. Moreover, he could not resume full-time work and study again for years. He stressed that the turning point in his own struggle to face life and his own limitations came when an American doctor advised him, "If you want to live to be one hundred years old, get an incurable disease and take care of it for the rest of your life!"

Another crucial challenge came from my own congregation. The vast majority of our leaders and members sent letters and get-well messages and prayers. Early, Mary had reported: "The church is paying your full salary while you are away. We have a wonderful supply pastor, Dr. Paul Preston, a friend of yours, an elder statesman and able preacher in our Brotherhood. Mr. Ellis and other key lay leaders want you to know that your pastorate will be waiting for you when you return, if you wish." Grateful for this trust, I could recall about five hundred members by name with enthusiasm.

On February 10th Mr. Howard Ellis, the Chairman of our Official Board, wrote:

> The wonderful reports of how well you are getting along are bringing a lot of happiness to a lot of people. . . . You just can't know how many people have been concerned about you and praying for just such reports as we are now receiving. . . . Dr. Preston fits our present situation like a warm sun. He never gives anyone an opportunity to forget that he is here for a short visit only.

One of the high-lights of my stay at Dix Hill was a visit from Mr. Ellis and Dr. Preston. They assured me: "The pulpit will be waiting for you when you get discharged and are rested. Whatever decision is made about your return, or how long to stay, will be entirely yours. The vast majority of the leaders and members want you as their pastor, when you are ready, if you so decide."

All the letters from the church either said or implied the same things. When I was at Graylyn, the church secretary, Miss Betty Yarbrough, wrote on December 17, 1953:

> "We have been missing you. . . . So many people have been calling and inquiring about you. And they all have offered their

services to help do anything they can. Mrs. West and the children are getting along fine. I have been going by to see them practically every day after work and some time during the evening. You would really be proud of every one of them. Lots of people have been visiting them and doing various things for them. . . . You have many friends here who are concerned about and who are pulling for you. You are remembered in our thoughts and prayers.

This was the kind of testimony that came from every source about the Hillyer Memorial Christian Church. It did much to relieve the pressure about my eventual return to society.

This was the obvious spirit of our congregation which I saw and felt on the few weekends when I was allowed to visit my home. The hospital staff granted me permission to attend the church's Sunday-morning worship services if I would take no official part. Dr. Preston asked me to greet members with him as they left the sanctuary after the services. I could sense how almost all the members and leaders felt about seeing me again, and their appreciation and respect. It was after those encounters that I decided to return to my pastorate, after my final release, to see if I could make the grade as a minister again. I desperately wanted the trial to be where I had originally cracked up, and among the same people.

I believed more than ever in democratic congregational church government; I believed that I would now be better qualified to understand and to adjust to my critics who opposed my efforts toward such a local church program. This had been the chief battle which added to the pressures leading to my nervous breakdown. I was again convinced that the new Functional Committee-Advisory Council organization program, which I had introduced in my new pastorate, was essential for the Disciples of Christ or Christian Churches to adjust their New Testament principles to modern culture and Christian growth, and for the health of leaders and members at the local church grass-roots level.

With these growing convictions, I believed I could set the necessary example by being, this time, a more democratic and tolerant minister and by sharing a deeper Christian spirit than I had exhibited before my crack-up. No longer did I blame my critics and enemies in the local church for my own failures and illness. Now I blamed only myself. And I believed that I was called of God to help set this needed example among my members and leaders, and that our local church was destined to pioneer in this new experiment recommended by nearly all of our denomination's leaders and scholars. "This time," I thought, "I shall combine the insights of the New Testament with democracy and the principles of sound mental and emotional health."

Before those church visits, I had my doubts about ever returning as a regular pastor. I knew that the entire weight of the State Hospital Staff was against my returning to Hillyer Memorial. One staff member put it this way: "Dr. West, you have too many bitter personal enemies within the church. The objective record shows that their treatment of previous ministers was too rugged for them to give you an adequate test with another chance to win them as friends."

But what the staff implied was nothing compared with my experience at an oyster roast held on the hospital grounds by the men of our church. (I was allowed to go to that gathering long before I made my first weekend visit to the parsonage and church.) Of course, I had no part on the program, but I could spot at a glance the obvious hostility of a few men. On the other hand, I could sense the joy, surprise, and deep loyalty of the vast majority present. The hugs, handshakes, and pleas of so many, saying, "Come back to be our preacher again when you are able; we miss you so much," were a comfort and challenge beyond measure.

In the long run, my doubts melted. I was convinced that there were a few leaders who resented me—perhaps rightly so—and who wanted their pound of flesh as well as the complete control of the church that they had had before I challenged their domination and monopoly. "But they don't represent the spirit and growing Christian vitality of the overwhelming majority of my leaders and members," I thought. "This problem of facing all critics and opposition has got to be licked within me, humbly, and in a Christian way. I may not think I am able to do it. But by God's grace I can and I shall!"

Letters from old tennis friends from many states increased the challenge of the outside world. One in particular helped me to feel accepted among my Carolina tennis companions. It came on March 28, 1954, from Whit Cobb, my successor as president of the Eastern Carolina Tennis Association, and one of the most respected athletes in the South. He had been honored as the "Athlete of the Year" in the old Southern Conference during his senior year at Davidson College. Whit wrote:

DEAR FRED,

I have been thinking about you quite a bit these last few weeks, not only in concern over your being in the hospital but also, "I wonder if Fred's going to play in the E.C.T.A. this year." The only guy I've ever known who didn't mind playing you, when he was in shape, is Lou Faquin. Yours truly never relishes the thought of having you on the other side of the net! . . .

Fred, all the fellows asked me to write you a sort of letter of appreciation as well as a general get-well from the E.C.T.A., as such, and in all sincerity I want to say on their behalf, you mean a great deal to us all and we hope things are going to be well with you soon. If there is anything you want any of us to do, you know that you only have to ask.

Get well soon, Fred, in plenty of time for the E.C.T.A. But, dammit, stay out of my half of the draw.

Very sincerely,
WHIT

Until I got such letters from tennis friends, I had never considered being able to play tennis again. Normal recreation was not the problem for me, in anticipating my return to society. The two burning questions were: "Should I risk the ministry again? Can I readjust myself to society again?"

More letters came than I could manage to read during my stay in the ward. I wanted to reply to each one, not out of conscious pride or duty, but gratitude. Unwilling to risk the frustration, I read only the letters from persons to whom I felt very close. I could answer only a fraction of them. The other mail I hoarded for future use. I resolved: "I might find the going tougher later, when I return to society. The temptation to retreat into my old shell might be too easy. I'll save these unopened letters and cards for such times. They may offer just the memories and comfort I shall need. Now my job is to take this insulin, not a correspondence course." But several big boxes of unopened mail added to my self-respect and confidence. Otherwise, I should have never dreamed that I had so many friends and well-wishers in the outside world.

However, my most vital inspiration was the Bible. I did not glance at the printed book while I was in the hospital. Having taught it for years, I studied choice passages and chapters from memory. While I was lying down, resting, certain passages spoke to my condition and deepest needs without any conscious effort of mine. I did not have to go to the Holy Scriptures; they came to me, of my very being and problems. I concluded: "This experience confirms anew my faith that God seems to choose His own mysterious ways, places, and times to speak to all sorts and conditions of men through the Scriptures and through events and people not usually regarded by society or churches as either sacred or conventional."

My final release to return to normal society came on May 14, 1954. This was the most exciting day of hospitalization since I had gone to Graylyn on November 14, 1953. I had longed for this impending day of freedom; but, privately, I had dreaded it also. It was more trying than I had imagined.

A few days earlier, an official of the hospital had a private appointment with me to break the news. He informed me of the possible date, assuming that my sixty comas would be completed by then. He said: "We have decided to make an exception in your case, if you prefer. Ordinarily, you would be kept here for some weeks for psychotherapy. But if you agree voluntarily to choose some qualified psychiatrist and undergo this discipline for your readjustments with him, we'll release you within twenty-four hours of your last coma. That should be Saturday, May 14th. Now what do you say?"

"Great!" I replied. "I'd like to have Dr. Richard Proctor at Graylyn, who was in charge of my case in the first place. Is that okay?"

"Yes," he responded. "He's a very able specialist. This should be a happy solution for you. We are afraid that keeping you here longer in this environment, without the company of enough people of your background and condition, might slow up your readjustments. Also, frankly, we do not have a psychiatrist available to handle your case as some of the staff think it ought to be. Dr. Young is qualified, and could do it, but he is too tied up with administration as a superintendent. You see, we are not accustomed to having someone with your background and reading knowledge of this field. Some of our psychiatrists might make an unintentional slip on almost any subject —take religion, for example. One such error might make you lose respect for his professional judgment and set you back—instead of helping you to face reality. In any case, we think that out-patient therapy with a specialist of your own choice will be wise in your situation."

He inquired, "By the way, do you think you are well?"

I said: "I don't know, Doctor. So far as I can tell, I am well. But how would I be qualified to know? I shall gladly accept whatever judgment and requests that Dr. Proctor makes."

"Good," he retorted. "That's all that is needed on your part. You don't think you're a psychiatrist, do you? I am not one myself. What is your opinion?"

"Of course I am not a psychiatrist, or any sort of specialist in this field," I answered.

"Good," he said. "I point this out to you now, for this was one of your symptoms. You assumed that you were a psychiatrist before your breakdown. You were in bad shape. You used to fear that your church enemies would destroy you by some secret devices through waves or what not over the radio or by other gadgets."

I left him, grateful for his spirit, admiring his usual kindness and frankness. But I was amused at his questions about my attitudes toward myself. I thought: "I wonder if nonprofessional people will tend to confuse symptoms of my disease with its real causes? There's no telling what I did think about myself during those blacked-out months. It's all Greek to me now. If these doctors don't know me or my health any better now than that, I'm lucky that Dr. Proctor will be in final charge of me. Otherwise, I might never get out of this place or have a chance to prove myself."

Saturday, May 14th, finally came. I found it hard to say goodbye to our ward. I said to myself: "Passing through the last locked door will be no gleeful celebration such as I've long imagined. Why does this approaching event remind me of my academic graduation ceremonies? We shall have no formal ceremonies, speeches, music, stirring Alma Mater, or colorful processions of caps and gowns. I've seen too many other patients leave this ward."

While awaiting word that my wife had come for me, I reflected: "I am glad to be able to leave, but concerned about my comrades who are still unable to. I have learned to love each one of them; I have been happy at every sign of progress each patient made. Also, don't I feel a sense of security here now that I am afraid to give up? I know the ropes now, in this ward and hospital, but God only knows what I've got to learn to reorient myself to home life and society again! Am I really afraid that I'll crack up again and be brought back to this place?"

Then I thought: "Why fear the unknown? I have learned to love, not merely to endure, my sick friends. Why can't I learn to love and live with even the most unlovely and miserable persons in the outside world too? If I have made my adjustments successfully to abnormal society, why can't I do the same in normal society? To heck with this stuff. Let's face greater reality, Fred, and get it over with!

"Maybe I'm in better shape to leave now than some of the other guys were. Being on legal probation for one year is no problem to me. Yet it was to others as they were ready to leave. I respect this law of the state. It's a good test of whether I am in as good shape as I have long believed I was. One year is plenty of margin to find out fully."

In this mood, I received my congratulations from the ward. Coming forward to shake hands and wish me luck, the patients seemed to have more joy and gaiety for my own sake than I did. They shared my happiness without trace of envy or jealousy.

An elderly attendant, Mr. J. D. Pipkin, approached, tears streaming down his rugged face. He cried: "Dr. West, it will never seem the same again to work in this ward without you around. You've made it such fun!" I was deeply moved by one of the kindest men I ever knew.

Another attendant, young Hampton Breedlove, came over to slap my back. He said: "Dr. West, you don't remember it, but I was with you in one of the other wards soon after you came to Dix Hill. That was before they put you in this insulin ward. And I was sure that, of all patients I ever saw at Dix Hill, you had almost the least chance of any to recover and leave. I am so proud of you! We are going to miss you more than words can say."

Another favorite attendant, Owen Ryals, shared his hopes and happiness. Two of our choice nurses, Mrs. Prandy Jackson and Mrs. Pansy Leonard (whom I had known at Atlantic Christian College and whom I called "Blondie"), had nice things to say about my being "a model patient" and a "joy to work with." The head nurse also was wonderful.

The word came: "Your wife has come! Don't hold her up. Your kids are in the car too. Go ahead, but be sure to come back and visit us and play some canasta with us."

Becoming an alumnus of State Hospital was no picnic. Leaving was one of my most profoundly reverent and humbling experiences. This was the greatest, yet strangest, Commencement Day of my career.

I did not rush to leave the old building. I lingered to pray quietly with my eyes open before the ward, thinking of "my little community." Although I was eager to see my wife and to go home with our children, I remained to talk with each patient. I thanked God for State Hospital, with all its limitations and weaknesses. I was grateful for its growing improvements, and for the grapevine's news that Dr. Walter Sikes, the superintendent-to-be as of July 1st, was up to date and would lead the hospital in needed reforms, improvements, and changes. I knew that this would take time, but my confidence in Dr. Sikes' foresight and concern for people had meant much to me for months. In addition, knowing that a new chapel was under way, as well as other new buildings, made me grateful.

I thanked God for His gifts of medical and mental sciences to help all sick human beings everywhere in His whole world. I asked God to bless all of the hospital's staff, patients, and wards. And I prayed that all nations and people in the outside world might be led to share the human kinship and mutual understanding which we had been guided to share gladly within our own locked ward. I praised God for showing me, even through this rugged means, what it is like for people in need to help "bear one another's burdens, thus fulfilling the law of Christ."

As we drove home, I prayed: "O God, an old way of life is being discarded again. A new way of life is about to begin. Be my Shepherd yet, lest I forget."

As we traveled, the sun appeared to shine and sparkle more radiantly than I had ever noticed before. The blue sky stretched like an endless open tent above stately trees robed in lovely spring shades of green with grass spreading from them like majestic carpets. Never had birds looked so graceful or sung with such sweetness. Flowers offered their full beauty, as though they, too, had nothing to hide or hold back. I prayed, "O God, how good and beautiful is your outside world, which holds back nothing of its mysteries and goodness. Guide me not to hold back any of Your image within me from You or from any man in this outside world. I am not ashamed of my illness, but grateful for it as the best blessing and discipline ever received to enrich and deepen my entire life."

I did not say much on the way home. It was sufficient to hear my wife and children talk. They all seemed to know just what to say or to leave unsaid—far better than I did.

When we did get home, I could not say much then, either. Everyone seemed to understand. But I did not. I asked myself: "Why does my family seem to understand how I feel better than I do? How do they know that all I crave for a while is to stretch out in my easy chair in the den? Or to hear mainly the glad voices and laughter of the children again? How does Mary Margaret, our older daughter, know that I expect to hear her play the piano?"

I noted carefully that none of the family seemed embarrassed to have me back home for good. No one acted as though any apology or regret was due about my illness and confinement. I was received as naturally as if I had never been away.

No one looked disappointed when I wanted to take a long nap after we got used to one another again. There was no pressure about losing time together or for me to leave the house for anything. This trip home, I did not eye the clock and count the fleeting minutes before having to leave again. After I had had a grand sleep, Mary's cooking tasted better than it had even during those unforgettable weekend visits home from the hospital. In fact, everything tasted better on May 14, 1954!

The first few days were no problem. I did not want to go anywhere. Even our meager yard looked marvelous to me. The once-prized little garden, now barren and weedy, offered an invitation to immediate spading and planting. And, to my surprise, friends did not phone or interrupt our family privacy. (I had dreaded hearing the incessant ringing of the phone again, day and night.)

Soon I began to read part of the big store of unopened personal letters I had brought back from Dix Hill. Before doing so, I decided against my earlier plans to have every laundry label with my name, with its obvious hospital stamp, removed from my clothes. I concluded: "After all, the hospital has made a lasting imprint upon my life and mind. Why try to rub its marks out of my clothes? Fred, be glad, not sad, for every reminder of the hospital's life and help."

During the first days of my return home as a free man, I was not ready for another graduation, nor did I even leave my house and family for a short walk. But I had passed the kindergarten and the first grade of my schooling in normal society again! The laundry stamps were my marks, and I accepted them with no feeling of uneasiness or injustice. The unopened letters and garden were my next assignments. And, when I got too tired at either task, I took a recess and nap any time I desired.

I decided: "My first test is to learn to live happily and naturally again with my own family. After that, I shall look beyond my own home, but through it, to face larger units of society in due time."

8

Making a Crucial Comeback

After a few days at home, I was sure that living a normal life again with my family would be natural and happy. I decided: "Like rowing a boat downstream, this will be no strain for me. I must watch ahead for rocks and rapids, fearing nothing behind."

Increasingly, I looked forward to the next eventful step to readjust myself to society: my first appointment with Dr. Proctor at Graylyn Hospital, in order to keep my promise to Dix Hill. This "honor system" appealed to me. I felt: "Dr. Proctor will know in one session whether I am completely well or not. I am prepared to accept his pronouncement or advice, no matter what it is."

My wife drove me to Graylyn for the engagement within a week of my return home. On the way to Winston-Salem she filled more gaps in my faulty recollection about having been a patient at Graylyn before going to State Hospital. I explained: "Mary, my impressions are few and foggy. I've forgotten what Dr. Proctor looks like. But I do recall the sound of his voice, his informal manner, and my respect and trust for him. I dimly recall a swimming pool, a tennis court, and a golf course there. I can also remember playing some basketball in a gym."

As we approached Graylyn, it appeared vaguely familiar. It did not resemble any hospital I had ever seen. A luxurious structure, it looked like an old, aristocratic country estate, semi-Victorian and ornate, well kept both inside and outside. Its grounds and facilities reminded me more of those of a modern country club.

I met Dr. Proctor. He smiled as if happy to see me. Shaking hands, he said: "Hello, Fred. I'm glad to see you again! You look fine. Come into my office and let's have a chat."

Prematurely bald, but young looking, he gave the impression that he could be happy and able in any profession or interest. He had the rare gift of being relaxed and completely at ease himself, thus making everybody else at ease with him. He seemed like the best friend I had ever known. My blocked memory was no handicap in his presence. I was thrilled because I could remember the sound of his voice.

My first reaction was: "I'm in a bigger league than I have been used to for months. He does not call me 'Dr. West' at all. No patient or staff member at Dix Hill ever called me 'Fred' except the chaplain and Dr. Sikes. Dr. Proctor doesn't make me feel like a museum piece, or like a prize exhibit among rare Ph.D. or ministerial failures on the Hill."

Before I could pursue this comparison further, Dr. Proctor asked me how I liked being home again with my family. He wanted to know how I was sleeping, eating, and whether or not I had any more headaches. Before I could raise my questions, he remarked: "Fred, you had a critical nervous breakdown that is typical of many ministers, doctors, lawyers, and business executives nowadays. This is a growing trend, especially among these professions. We have many ministers who have breakdowns and come to Graylyn. They do very well when they return to their pastorates. In popular language, we call your illness a 'professional disease.' "

Silently, I thought: "This makes more sense than everything I was told at State Hospital. And it's in line with what their best psychiatrist called 'a high-grade nervous breakdown' in my case."

Before our short session ended, I was amazed. I had planned to ask many questions, but Dr. Proctor answered them all before I could raise them. Though I had the feeling that he was reading my mind, this did not make me feel awkward or self-conscious. Unlike my previous experiences on the Hill, he did not waste time mentioning, much less expounding, problems that I had long overcome. Nor did he equate former symptoms of my illness with their more profound and complex causes. His understanding of the work of the ministry was subtle and practical; this was challenging and evident.

Before I left, he declared: "Fred, you are fully recovered and 100 per cent well technically. Now your remaining hurdle is to complete your readjustment to regular society. This you must do, step by step, without any risk of getting too tired or of straining yourself. Insulin shock treatments are exhausting. You are worn down physically. You need to rest and build up before you resume a normal load of work with your church again. How would you like to take a month's vacation with Mary and your children to rest up? You could do no better than to fish, swim, and sleep all you want."

"Wonderful," I replied. "I'll be glad to do so. I understand that our church leaders want me to take any vacation desirable and to wait as long as I wish before preaching again. I'd love to do it."

"Swell," he said. "Why don't you folks go tó Florida or some such place for a month? Then check back here and let me see how you are getting along. If you feel up to it by then, you might be ready to return to your pulpit on the first Sunday of July. But I wouldn't do any visiting or attend any church gatherings. Let's see how that works. Get used to preaching first; then you can gradually take on a few more of your ministerial duties."

When I left his office, he invited Mary to come in "for a little talk." In the waiting room, I reviewed our conversation, respecting, his advice and accepting his judgment. I was happy. The session had been like an enjoyable informal visit with a friend. In amusement, I told myself: "Dr. Proctor doesn't hide his genuine personality and love of life behind a mask of technical terms and psychiatric lingo to prove that he is an informed psychiatrist. Like Ted Williams, he doesn't have to carry a baseball bat in a subway to prove he's big league. Nor does he talk as though he is reciting class lectures or rehashing old research notes. He simply talks, and talks simply. Any child could understand him, yet recognize his humility and the authentic insight behind what he says."

What challenged me most, however, was Dr. Proctor's explanation of my "sudden and complete recovery." Like the specialists at Dix Hill, he felt that it could not "be explained adequately in scientific terms." Several of them had told me that this experience was "mysterious, and beyond our scientific understanding and knowledge." But Dr. Proctor had used the word "miraculous."

I pondered: "Could this expert suspect anything about my experience at Dix Hill which cannot be known, and could not have been reported, by anyone else but me? I wonder if I would respect him as highly as I do if he did not understand the limitations of any one field of learning to explain and master all fields of life and learning. Obviously I am guided now by no ordinary psychiatrist. Dr. Proctor is not the son of a minister for nothing! He is one specialist who really knows something about his own training and religion combined. And he has personal humility, too."

I thought: "Whatever else a miracle really is, I have experienced one, if not many. God has surely produced a miracle through medical and psychiatric sciences and my own background. Perhaps some of God's greatest miracles and revelations today come through the hands and skills of gifted people who are seldom, if ever, aware that they are God's servants or that their daily work and professions glorify God whether they know it or not. Funny thing: I used to think of miracles as linked only with ages and cultures in the distant past. Perhaps my original sense of awe and mystery was diminished, not enhanced, by reason and knowledge and 'sophisticated' faith derived from my own inner weaknesses as a human being."

Mary, the children, and I spent a happy month on the Gulf Coast at Pass-A-Grille Beach, Florida. We enjoyed the pleasant vacation-resort home of the Weldon Osbornes who were intimate friends of my brother Bill in Chattanooga, Tennessee. Their personal concern that we be their guests for as long as we wished to vacation both in 1954 and in 1955 was a major factor in my readjustment to society. This hospitality in Florida offered us an ideal retreat from society to be to ourselves as an intimate family.

There I discovered that I could meet and deal with strangers in small groups without being self-conscious. My brother George, a minister and the state secretary of our Christian Churches in Tennessee, joined us for a couple of weeks. We did a great deal of fishing. Before George left, I had learned to handle the rowboat by myself without tiring too much, and I could fish alone with confidence. At first I was unable to row as I had years before.

The only tough problem that I faced during the vacation was the long wait on the beach before I finally got the courage to enter the water, much less to try to swim. The first time in, I had to dive; I could not force myself to wade into the water gradually. With this experience, I found that I had to relearn almost every old habit except one—driving an automobile, which felt natural at the first attempt. But when I was driving I was no longer in a hurry. I was surprised to find that my major lack of confidence was not merely in meeting people. I had anticipated that difficulty for months. But I had to relearn to do practical things, no matter how sound the habits had been before.

Before leaving Florida, I exchanged letters with some of my ward comrades back in Raleigh. It was a joy to keep up with their progress, having visited them before I left for the vacation. On June 22nd Bennie (B. O.) Slaughter wrote, addressing me as "Fred" for the first time:

DEAR FRED:

So you're leaving Saturday to fill the canasta date? Fine! We'll certainly be on the lookout, and it will be good to see you and your tan.

Sterling "graduated" today—M'Gee yesterday. . . . We still reside at Royster—they're as slow at moving to the new building as they are relinquishing holding to the theory of 60 comas to "guarantee" cure. . . . I am now approaching that "magic" 50— today was No. 46.

I know now why you recovered slower in the last 15—I'm getting where I am the last one out almost every day. Just lay after the orange juice and can't get my bearings—One day I had showered—washed, put on underwear and was eating breakfast and couldn't remember at all having showered or washed—but I had, they said.

The boys all send greetings, and best wishes. We will be awaiting your return with keen anticipation of seeing evidence of much progress in your health and good looks. Until then, this is Station BOS signing off with a request that you convey to your family our regards.

Sincerely,
BENNIE

On the trip back to Raleigh, the children were astonished that I kept offering to let Mary drive. I had had to let her help on the way down to Pass-A-Grille because I got too tired to drive after each two-hour stretch. But I was physically in better shape, tanned and stronger, although I still had an embarrassing amount of what the Hill called "excess insulin fat." (Dix Hill specialists predicted that I would lose most of this extra weight "within a few weeks out of the hospital," but it was many months in my case.) The family reminded me that before my illness I had insisted on doing all the driving on long trips and would not trust the car to my wife without becoming tense and jittery whenever she blew the horn or applied the brakes.

Jesting, I claimed: "Children, your mother has really changed. She has learned to be a good driver while I was away—that is, for a woman."

They chuckled, and replied, "No, Daddy, you're the one that has changed, not Mommy." I was convinced during that month's trip that both my wife and I had changed immensely. Little problems which used to make for tensions, and even major difficulties, between us we now took in stride.

Upon our return home, I found that my relearning process was going on in nearly every realm of life. What others took for granted as simple things were now vaguely, strangely familiar. I knew the main buildings, landmarks, and streets of Raleigh, but I had to learn anew the map of Raleigh, and untold numbers of streets and places which I used to know by heart. All of this took energy and concentration; much of it at a time was tiring.

While rediscovering how to do practical things and to relearn the city on drives with the family, I tried little reading. I found that I could not use my mind much without becoming exhausted and drowsy. Mary and the children seemed to welcome and understand these new trends in my life. I never had to explain these problems to them, for they seemed to understand, and usually pointed to and described once-known things without my asking.

When Mary and I returned to Graylyn within a few days, Dr. Proctor seemed pleased with my progress. He gave me the green light to preach again on the first Sunday of July if I "felt up to it" and if I would undertake no other ministerial work until I felt "completely at home again in the pulpit." He stressed: "Fred, you'll learn how to pace yourself in time. You mustn't risk getting too tired or ever bite off more than you can chew. You'll have to learn to detect your own warning signals for yourself. But, first, you simply want to take on one thing at a time. Entering the pulpit again will be your first big step. Come to see me in about a month so that we can check on how you are doing and consider some more steps to add gradually."

We went back to Raleigh to prepare for this crucial test. For weeks I had been sure that I could preach my first sermon again with confidence and enthusiasm—not because of any sense of duty or pressure from society, but because I felt that I had a fresh faith worth sharing. I had some deeper convictions about God's goodness, love, mercy, and hope for restless, weary, and discouraged humanity. But as the first Sunday of July approached, I felt the tensions and pressures multiplying. More and more, I knew that this would be the greatest test of my new life, faith, and health.

As formerly, I prepared my prayers and worship service before working on the sermon. But I tired fast. It took days to do these things. By Saturday, I felt sure that my prayers and sermon were for the congregation as a whole. To me, they were not private, subjective, and introspective. I went to sleep on Saturday night feeling certain that the pressure was off and that I had done my best in spiritual, moral, and emotional preparation for the next morning's "D-Day" test.

However, I woke up early Sunday morning feeling as I had when awaiting an insulin shock treatment, and at the exact hour I had begun our hospital routine for it. My confidence was gone. I asked: "How dare I preach again to this congregation? Most of them ought to preach to me. None of them has failed as much as I. And what if I get emotionally upset and go to pieces again from the same pulpit as I did only eight months ago? If so, would I be aware of it this time? Would it end my ministry?"

I went to the office early. I wanted to think and pray over these problems privately. I sat down, weeping. Feeling weary and defeated, I told myself: "Maybe I should call the whole deal off. I have a good alibi now. Everybody will say, 'Fred simply tried to do it too soon, before he was strong enough again.' But to do that would not be honest, just, or right; others would be deceived and I would only try to deceive myself again. Now I know what part of the trouble is: *I am just plain afraid!* I don't want to admit, even to myself, that my self-confidence and self-respect are not fully regained. Yet I am trembling with fear and anxiety."

97

Then I recalled how I had faced fright at crucial times in the hospital. I had learned to admit to myself and to confess to God that I was full of fear and was not self-sufficient to face myself, much less other people. I recalled: "Before my breakdown, the very words *courage* and *victory* were the most priceless and sacred words I knew. My former reputation in sports, the ministry, and academic life for 'guts' is merely a myth and legend to me now. I had believed in this personal tradition—and so had many of my friends and enemies.

"Yet, recently, *fear and defeat*, and an honest recognition of them, led me through the rugged paths toward a height of self-understanding and recovery. I had better pray."

I prayed. But not, as I often did before my breakdown, for more courage, faith, and success. Now I prayed, humbly and self-critically, for God's wisdom, understanding, mercy, and forgiveness. I said: "O God, I have betrayed the highest that I learned during my hospitalization. I have assumed again that, if I were simply to try hard enough, everything would come out all right." And I thanked God afresh "for making fear real and for making my own weaknesses disturb me." I did not ask for extra faith, but for God to "use the little new faith that has been a big part of my growing life."

Prayer and meditation merged until my burdens lifted and my tears were dried. I rethought every crucial decision I had ever made about the ministry: how I had never consciously wanted to be a preacher or a scholar as such, but had yearned that the Gospel be preached; and how I desperately needed to learn more about the world in which I lived in the light of Christ, the prophets, and the saints. I felt called into the ministry, not from conscious personal ambition, but because I dared not do anything else with my life. I was impelled to preach and to teach from a Will higher and deeper than my own haunting needs. I had no magical experiences, hearing no audible voices as this clear decision came. But God had spoken within my depths and conscience. My insatiable interest in scholarship had come consciously from a curiosity and a thirst to know more, not to be a scholar as such. Only in the hospital did I realize how complex these understandings were, and how profoundly I was involved in the original sin of mankind, as an individual.

I reflected: "Before I entered the ministry, I never felt worthy to be a follower of Christ, much less a minister of Christ. But in the ministry I got the illusion that I had become both a true follower and a worthy minister! Now I do not deserve the chance to preach again from the pulpit in which I broke down. No, I am not worthy of it at all. But by God's grace I am here. So by God's grace and the new faith He gave me, I'll see this sermon and service through!"

In this spirit, I found that I no longer wanted to run away. By that time, only a few minutes were left before the service was to begin. Several lay leaders came to the office, waiting silently but with confident smiles. I asked myself: "Do they know that if they speak I might cry? Do they know what it means to me when they merely smile, nod their heads, and lay their hands on my head and shoulders? If these friends believe in me, perhaps the congregation can tolerate my inadequate message!"

Ready, I went to the chancel. The thrill of my life came as the congregation rose to sing the processional hymn when I entered the sanctuary. I was overcome with gratitude at the attendance. I observed to myself: "So many of them are here, and on one of the poorest Sundays of the summer for normal attendance. Most of them look as if they are in private prayer as much as I am and have been. Perhaps they really are praying for their preacher. Thank God!"

Tears came to my eyes as I shared the Call to Worship and the Invocation. My voice tended to tremble. My tongue seemed so big that it choked me a few times while I read the Scriptures. I thought: "I had not thought before that I might personally identify myself with the passages involved. Why did this selection not seem so personal and subjective when I chose it?"

Early in the worship service, I faltered several times and almost stopped. This was the deepest emotional experience of my life in public worship. Then came the Lord's Supper, and I forgot about myself. Keeping my eyes on the Cross of Christ on the Lord's Table, I thought only of Him and His Gospel and forgiveness. Finally, I decided: "He is calling even a person like me to witness in His behalf." Fear and courage were no longer a problem, nor was I. No longer did I feel fear of sentimentality; but I was profoundly grateful for the kindness and prayers of my congregation and for my new vocation. Thus I, a new kind of minister, entered the pulpit and preached with all my heart, mind, and soul for God's glory and human faith—more assured than ever that these were the Church's fundamental mission and message for all sorts and conditions of men, including me.

The big test over, I was happy and poised as I greeted the congregation as beloved friends, when they left the building. They lingered to share warm words of welcome for my return. I was deeply, but not tearfully, thrilled to meet them as their regular pastor again, and I knew then that my emotions were profoundly healthy, genuine, and normal.

A week later, my next big test came, the second sermon of my "comeback." That service was almost as trying as the first until after the Lord's Supper. But God's grace through Christ was sufficient for me to be less awkward and self-conscious. And there was considerable, but less, strain during the third Sunday's service. Since then, there has never been such pressure on me before or during a worship service anywhere.

Happy and grateful beyond words, I felt that we all had done this together, with real teamwork and in Christian kindness. I could not have done it alone—without my family, the congregation, and without God's understanding and mercy. Nor could we have done it

16854

without the guidance, direct and indirect, of the skill and facilities of the technical experts; nor would it have been possible without Dr. Proctor's profound and practical understanding of organized religion.

The topics of those first three sermons are revealing. In order they were: "A Light in Darkness," "The Fullness of Christ," and "Pour Out Your Faith."

One new, unofficial tradition got its start among our key lay leaders during these three critical experiences involving the pulpit and public worship. Several of our men, of keen Christian insight and growing spiritual life, got in the habit of laying their hands firmly upon my shoulders or head as they filed by before I entered the sanctuary. And some still do so before a worship service, rarely saying a word.

This new ritual has remained sacred, strengthening our local congregation. It still makes me reevaluate the New Testament and Christian traditions of the power of God's Holy Spirit being channeled through the "laying on of hands." Who knows?

The wider the circle of our finite human knowledge and understanding becomes, the more the outer circle of mystery, which encloses it, expands and extends into the Infinite and Eternal.

9

The Road Back Toward Acceptance

Another crisis in my early readjustments came in August, 1954. I served as an official delegate of the Christian Churches (Disciples of Christ) at the Second Assembly of the World Council of Churches at Evanston, Illinois. This was like taking a bear by the tail, but beyond measure it accelerated my adjustment to normal life.

Until shortly before the assembly, the decision was postponed as to whether I was to attend, or resign my appointment as an official delegate. Our denomination's leadership took the position that the decision should be left to me. Typically, as early as March 19th, the executive secretary of the Disciples of Christ wrote to Mary:

DEAR MRS. WEST,

Thank you for the letter of March 9 reporting Fred's continued improvement. We are happy to know that you are still planning to be at Evanston and we know that if there is any change in your plans that you will notify us promptly. Otherwise, we are holding the credentials and reservations. . . .

We will be glad to hear from you or Fred himself at any time.

Cordially,

GAINES M. COOK

This was also the spirit shown by Dr. George Walker Buckner, Jr., the editor of *The World Call*, our international Christian magazine.

Dr. Buckner, the leading ecumenical statesman of our movement, was encouraging too, and his personal letters meant much to us.

Once the test of being able to preach again had been met, I felt sure that I should go to Evanston, if Dr. Proctor approved. I had known other ministers, who had had less severe breakdowns, who could not complete their first sermons during their first three Sundays back in their pulpits. I kept asking myself: "Why the number *three* in so many cases? And why suddenly was my fourth sermon as natural for me to preach as ever? Even the topic of my fourth sermon, 'No East or West in Christ,' is objective in spirit, or the word West would have choked me up. In any case, if I can face my congregation like this again, I can meet any test that Evanston offers me."

During my follow-up appointment at Graylyn, Dr. Proctor asked: "Fred, how would you like to go to Evanston? You've already met your first test in the return to your ministry in Raleigh. It will do you good to get away for the two weeks. I understand that you have been appointed as a delegate to the World Council Assembly and that the position is still open for you. The final decision as to whether to undertake it or not is yours. I personally think that the trip and experience will do you a lot of good now, that is, if you really want to go and feel up to it. You'll meet old friends. You'll learn a lot to help you in your work and build confidence."

"Wonderful," I replied. "I feel that I can do it now."

He said: "If you decide to go, be sure to go by airplane. In fact, I think you ought to take all your long trips by air from now on for a long time. It will be easier on you than going by car or train. But just be sure not to overdo yourself. Attend only what you feel you can without getting too tired. Then rest. If I were you, I would keep up my habit of lying down to rest for about forty-five minutes after lunch, whether you need to sleep or not. You may want to keep up this voluntary discipline for years to come."

I was delighted to go, and especially to meet the test of taking the trip alone. However, as our flight neared Chicago I became jittery and felt a cold sweat. I was afraid. I asked myself: "Will these Christian leaders accept or reject me? Those who don't know me may be wonderful. But how about my former friends and colleagues? Will they shun me? And those who don't know—will they realize that I have been in a mental hospital? What will my friends say when they see my twenty-six extra pounds of insulin-sugar fat? Why, in Heaven's name, did I think I was ready for this trip?"

But being at Evanston boosted my confidence, inspiration, and convictions. I reflected: "I've never seen such Christian power and fellowship shared from all over the world." To my surprise, I found that I could do the reading assignments. I kept up with all the major sessions and group discussions, fulfilling my role as delegate as though nothing had ever happened. I learned to pace myself, resting between meetings and appointments. From the start, it was a joy to meet old friends and comrades from other denominations and from my own movement, as well as from Yale. I soon felt at ease and at home. Moreover, I visited much with my two brothers, who took turns rooming with me for a week during the two-week assembly.

At Evanston I discovered that I could do creative writing again. Early, before breakfasts, I wrote my half of a postponed booklet. My brother William and I had long planned to write a little work together on "Who Are the Christian Churches and What Do We Believe?" To my surprise and happiness, I completed all of my part of the writing from memory, using no notes. (Since its publication more than 25,000 copies have been used by our religious movement.)

A chance chat with Dr. D. Elton Trueblood especially encouraged me further. We reviewed our grand times together before I had moved to the Tarheel State, especially the work, years before, in California on a volume for the Interseminary Movement's series of books, the seminar we had taught together at Wabash College in

Indiana, and how he had been instrumental in getting me the pro-
fessorship at that fine liberal-arts school. Dr. Trueblood shared more
personal, spiritual, and moral insight into my struggles with illness
and readjustments than did any other friend at Evanston. His sensitive Quaker spirit and his own experience with his physically stricken
wife qualified him to share in this way as few could. He was the
only Christian leader at Evanston who frankly raised the subject and
discussed my illness without caution.

Professor Trueblood stressed: "Fred, this experience need not be
a tragedy or handicap in your life. It may turn out to be the deepest
blessing of your entire career. God teaches us much through suffering, doesn't He? He enables us better to penetrate the struggles and
inner tensions of others through these personal struggles of our own.
I believe, Fred, that this detour may lead you to a deeper, fuller, and
more Christ-like ministry than could have been possible without it.
It did bring you closer to God. God is more vital, real, and inescapable than ever before, is He not? Prayer is a more vital part of your
daily life and normal decisions, I feel sure. Who knows? God may be
calling you to a more nearly unique vocation than could have otherwise been possible."

Accidental encounters with Dean Liston Pope of Yale also helped
me to realize that the former illness would be no lasting handicap
in academic and church circles. The dean was unusually kind, at
ease, and appreciative of my struggle to make a comeback. In his
gracious way, when I was alone at lunch one day, he insisted that I
join him with his roommate, Alan Paton. I wanted to tell the admired author: "Your novel *Cry, the Beloved Country* helped me
profoundly when I reread it during my illness. And I cannot express
how my hospital reading of your *Too Late the Phalarope* strengthened me." But I did not try. I thought, "He may think that I am
just 'apple-polishing him.'" It meant enough to me to swap jokes
and to share views about current social trends with these great
Christian prophets.

I was also inspired by the personal humility and kindness of Dr. Toyohiko Kagawa, of Japan. During a lunch with him at Evanston, we had one of the most inspiring conversations of my life. I told him: "When I was struggling for a greater faith and purpose in life as a student at Lynchburg College, I was assigned to review your book *A Grain of Wheat*. It made a vital impact upon my life." He appeared moved that his "little book was of such help to a college student in America." Then he told me about one of his major experiments in Japan: the planting of pecan trees "to help poor families make a more productive use of unpromising soil." He believed that "this might help the whole economy and way of life of Japan."

This reminded me of Trueblood's illustration about the countless people who had lost their way in the voyage of life—without rudder or compass: "Folks who learn to give themselves to causes which are bigger than themselves, and which will outlast their own brief span of existence, are already on the way toward finding meaning and significance in their lives." Trueblood had said, "One who plants a shade tree, knowing full well that he will never live to sit in its shade is, himself, an evidence of immortality."

For months to come, I pondered this experiment of Kagawa and his concern to do as Jesus did, to help feed the poor and dignify all human life. Also, I recalled the humbling experience of being seated next to Kagawa at an assembly session, and how disturbed he was that I did not have a copy of the printed program. He lent me his copy, which he had been holding only a few inches from his extra-thick glasses, insisting that I read it before he did. This man, almost blind from a disease of the eyes, reminded me of how Jesus took a towel and girded himself and washed his own disciples' feet. I silently accepted this act as a personal example for my own life.

At Evanston, I could tell at a glance any acquaintances who were aware of my breakdown and were awkward in my presence. I did not resent this response. I thought: "Not a person treats me as though I have had tuberculosis or some fatal contagious disease. The few who are awkward are embarrassed because they do not know how sensitive I am about my illness; they simply do not know if they should mention the subject." I enjoyed putting them at ease by talking with them as though nothing had happened. At the other extreme, when friends were eager to know more about my experience and progress, I felt perfectly free to answer all questions frankly and to share my gratitude for having had an illness from which I had learned so much. This was particularly true in the case of Dr. W. A. Welsh, the pastor of East Dallas Christian Church. We had been professors together at Texas Christian University. We spent much time together.

Another personal encounter at Evanston helped me, above all, to realize that I had fully regained my healthy sense of humor in a new, self-critical light. One noted delegate, a marvelous Christian spirit and a hail-fellow-well-met, coaxed me aside from a group of close friends. I had been with him many times individually and in group discussions at the assembly, but he was not aware that I was the person who had had the breakdown. Lowering his voice, he asked anxiously: "Dr. West, how *is* your brother? I am so concerned about him! I heard about that terrible nervous breakdown he had. How is he progressing?"

Amused, I kept a poker face and whispered: "Don't talk so loudly! There's George, right over there. He might hear us, and he's very sensitive about the whole setback. Let's not hurt his feelings!"

Though the Evanston assembly was crucial in the trends of worldwide Christianity, it was also the turning point in my own new life. In addition to what I have described, the trip and encounters taught me that I should no longer dread to face crowds, strangers, or old friends.

These fears disappeared forever. During my return to Raleigh, I thought: "I've mixed and talked with strangers at the airports. Travelers treated me as they did everyone else. Most friends acted as though nothing had ever happened, and I was not at all embarrassed." When I got home, I knew that this crucial personal battle with my inner self had been won. I told myself: "Now I have learned anew that I am always my own biggest enemy! The social struggle is within me. I distrusted society only because I distrusted myself. From now on, I shall no longer be sensitive about what society might do, say, or think about my present and future status as one who has been seriously ill mentally." This hardest lesson of all for an ex-patient was learned once for all.

Back in Raleigh, ministerial friends were kind and understanding beyond words. Especially helpful were Dr. Edwin McNeill Poteat and Father John Dillon. Dr. Poteat, the pastor of Pullen Memorial Baptist Church, guided the Raleigh Ministerial Association, of which I was the vice president, in special prayers for me when I became ill. As their president, he sent the group's lovely flowers to my wife with the report of the concerned prayers and confidence of our fellow clergymen. Dr. Poteat was the first minister to hail my return and to provide the intimate fellowship that only ministers can have. We had long been friends, but now we were as close as kinsmen. And we shared life and faith together, as few could, until his untimely death. This witty, gay, but profoundly serious saint, scholar, musician, poet, and athlete was joy to my soul and light for my path.

Father John Dillon, a Roman Catholic priest and intimate tennis friend, was next to Dr. Poteat in personal encouragement and comradeship. He was one of the first clergymen to phone me, to visit, and to let me know that he had prayed for me and had believed that I would fully recover. He often stressed that he had "a close friend, a priest, who traveled over the same road and had made his comeback, a wiser and better man."

The Raleigh ministers who helped me with understanding and faith are too many to name. I mention only Dr. Howard Powell, minister of the Edenton Street Methodist Church; Dr. James Dick, rector of the Church of the Good Shepherd; the Reverend Edward

Agsten, pastor of the West Raleigh Presbyterian Church; Dr. James Beckwith, rector of St. Michael's Episcopal Church; and Dr. James Sprunt, the minister of First Presbyterian Church.

But the Raleigh parsons who were of the deepest personal help I can describe but not name. They were those active preachers who had similar breakdowns themselves, before coming to Raleigh or since. However, this is not known by their churches or by the public, except in two cases. Psychiatrists had told me who some of them were. Others phoned me confidentially, sharing their faith from their own personal experience. And a few whispered their stories to me at public gatherings, but asked me not to reveal their identities. The general public knows of their cases as "operations," "heart attacks," "ulcers," "physical breakdowns," and "rests from overwork."

Merely knowing personally so many able ministers who were ex-patients, now serving or having once served churches in our capital city, was consoling. This knowledge made me realize: "I am no rare case among local clergymen, even if the public thinks I am. And I have more freedom than most of these clergymen to make a personal witness as a former patient. I do not have to conceal my way of life or to suffer a false sense of guilt and shame, fearing that the public might find out about my mental illness."

Tennis friends welcomed my return to the courts. In fact, I was playing tennis again before I left for Evanston. I was too fat and relaxed to do well, but a tennis racket was one of the few things for which I had not lost the "feel." And I had learned not to mind defeats as long as I could still play the game. Tennis was now a sport; not an obsession, but a joy.

My congregation was wonderful. The vast majority were gracious, kind, and understanding; so were our lay leaders. I was aware of a few who were self-conscious and awkward in my presence when I was released from the hospital. They never changed, nor were they willing to find that I had changed. But most members had changed their conception of the role of a minister and of their roles as lay-

109

men, much as I had. This made readjustments to my work and flock natural, and Dr. Proctor's advice less difficult to follow.

None of our respected leaders and influential members expected me to work and serve beyond my human limitations. Their pressure was in the opposite direction, urging me to resume my duties gradually and not to "overdo." As a new man, I not only was a new minister in a new role, but faced a new congregation and lay leadership. While I had grown, my congregation had grown in self-understanding and self-criticism.

This was no accident. Alert members realized that their local church had a unique history. Two young ministers, well trained, had had nervous breakdowns in succession. Our members asked, not "Why did our minister go to pieces?" but "Why have we had two *in a row* to do so? Did we add to their pressures when we might have shared their load?"

Another crucial event occurred before my last session with Dr. Proctor. With his permission, I attended the Disciples of Christ International Convention at Miami in October, 1954. There I had many encounters similar to those at Evanston. But at Miami I was entirely among the leaders and friends of my own religious communion. I knew more people; my duties were lighter; my schedule was freer.

However, one new, unanticipated trend emerged at Miami which made me ponder a new role for my life. Numbers of ministers, wives, and others asked for personal conferences. They were concerned about impending nervous breakdowns among themselves or their loved ones. They frankly begged for advice, asking about some problems and experiences of mine that might guide their own decisions.

I talked with them at hotels, convention places, on streets, during meals, at the beach and while fishing. This intimate, personal type of witnessing was easy, and without strain. I appreciated this new response of others out of their own needs, and spent more time at this work than in regular convention activities. I sought out no one for these personal sessions; all approached me voluntarily, representing every region in the United States. Most of them were from ministerial families, but by the close of the convention laymen were coming too.

They all seemed so grateful, but I was unaware of being of any real help. I had merely shared some personal experiences and impressions, stressing bits of advice which Dr. Proctor had given both me and my wife, individually.

Little did I realize then that this was only the beginning of a new trend in my ministry! In a few months letters and people would be coming to me from all over North Carolina and from other states for such personal sharing. Nor did I believe that doctors, ministers, and psychiatrists would ever deliberately send troubled people to me, of all persons. I had no pattern of techniques or style of sharing; I had only a personal story and some impressions that I had gained from it.

However, when I returned from Miami I was convinced: "My readjustments must be maturing normally and fully. Otherwise, why do other people come to me for help and advice?" This two-way process helped me more than it could have helped others. They believed in me more than I did. And I believed in them more than they believed in themselves.

10

A New Life in a New Ministry

In early December, 1954, I had another big test to face: another graduation. This involved my seventh and final monthly session with Dr. Proctor since my discharge from State Hospital. This conference ended my psychotherapy. Making his decision, Dr. Proctor said, "Fred, your readjustments are 100 per cent. We would be wasting time to have more sessions. However, if you ever need to talk with me, be sure to let me know. Good luck!"

Dr. Proctor had taught me some rules of living which I could apply for the rest of my life. He had given me the green light gradually to resume a full schedule for my daily work, the kind that every normal adult should have. He left no detailed map or blueprint for my life, but a new kind of diploma: the lasting imprint of self-understanding, confidence, self-respect, and voluntary self-discipline.

All along he had cautioned me, "Don't bite off more than you can chew," in increasing my work, recreation, and social life. He urged me to take all the physical exercise I wanted, including tennis; to read according to my growing ability and interest, and to do some more visiting, but not too much. He warned, "It will be your job to learn to detect your own warning signs of fatigue and strain, and to learn to do what you believe you ought to do as long as it is not harmful to others or to yourself."

At the last session Dr. Proctor gave me clearance to hold funerals and weddings, and to do some limited counseling again. Until then, I was restricted from trying much more than regular visits to the hospitals about twice a week, sermonizing, and a minimum of office work. He assured me, "You are now ready to resume a normal schedule. But be sure to pick it up gradually; rest amply, and keep up your regular forty-five-minute afternoon naps or periods in which to lie down and relax."

I had enjoyed these monthly sessions with him, as had my wife, with whom he always had short follow-up chats. Also, Mary and I delighted in the trips together to and from Winston-Salem. After the final appointment, I kept thinking: "Now he's kicking me out of the nest. Can I learn to fly well enough alone? Perhaps I can, if I keep reviewing what I have learned from him."

Returning to Raleigh, I tried to summarize the few basic principles he had shared. One was a session about my loss of memory. Dr. Proctor asked: "Fred, why should your loss of memory for parts of a three- to six-month period bother you? What difference would it make in your life now or in the future if you were to know every detail that is blanked out of your mind now? You can't change the past, can you?"

"No," I replied.

"Even God cannot change the past, can He?"

"No," I said. "God cannot change what has already happened."

"Then do you really want to be able to do what God himself does not have the power to do, Fred?" he inquired humbly. "But you can do something about the present. And you, like everybody else, can do something about your life and decisions in the future. Let's do what we can, and not worry or bother about what is beyond our own capacity to do!

"You see, your loss of memory is a blessing, not a handicap. If you ever really need to remember something that happened during that interval that escapes your memory now, it will come back to you. But, whatever else you do about it, do not try to force your memory. The harder you try, the more you will block it, and the more fatigued you will get. And whatever you do recapture will not make any difference in your readjustments to life as you now live it, and shall live it, anyway."

This approach solved the once vexing problem of amnesia for me. Furthermore, it seemed more realistic than the several schools of thought which Dix Hill had left me confused about, such as: "When you really get well, your memory will be restored fully"; or "There are several conflicting schools of thought about amnesia, and I don't know what to suggest."

As we reached the city limits, I told myself: "Among the favorite sayings that Dr. Proctor has repeated to me, I especially like these in regard to making decisions: *Never cross any bridges until you get to them;* this is a healthy personal tonic to transcend needless worry, anxiety, fears, and insecurity. I must *never try to burn my candle at both ends,* or I'll lose in a hopeless race again to exceed my own natural and acquired human limits. God has given me the same twenty-four hours a day that he has given everybody else. *Remember always that you are only one human being, not God Almighty, and that all other people are only human beings with their limitations too.* This third principle I must learn to obey voluntarily also, or my health and life will be lost in trying to cross bridges that are not there or in extinguishing what light God has let shine in my own darkness."

More deeply than ever, I realized that these basic principles are stressed, demonstrated, and proved throughout the Bible. I thought: "In different words and settings, God's Word beyond the written words of the Holy Scriptures speaks these truths in every age to all sorts and conditions of people. I must continue to learn to apply the insight of the New Testament Christians, just as Dr. Proctor so often stressed, in a *day by day existence.* This makes the teachings and example of Jesus intensely realistic and personal for me. From now on, I'll learn not to be 'anxious about tomorrow' or about myself, or about others whose decisions I cannot make for them. Concerned and responsible, yes, but not overanxious! And I must forever be aware that no man can live by himself alone any more than he can live by bread alone. Surely the insights of religion and psychiatry have a common source in facing reality, and they come from the ground of all being and reality. This ultimate ground of existence is God, the Creator, Judge, and Redeemer of all mankind in and beyond history."

I told Mary: "I have studied under a few of the great Biblical scholars of this century. Now I find that life is more than study, and any person is more than a student and more than a slave of his occupation, or else he loses and mars the image of God in his human dignity, health, service, and daily living. How odd it is that it took the nonspecialists of the Scriptures and of the history and thought of the Church to lead me to understand the Bible so personally and self-critically! Dr. Proctor himself is no technical Biblical or religious scholar, but he has the needed insight. Above all others, his help has enabled me to apply my Christian faith to life and reality in more vivid and personal ways than I had dreamed.

"All the good, the true, and the beautiful which I had learned during my previous life and study are not lost. They became distorted, twisted, shattered, and buried when I got them all out of focus—when I was blindly and unconsciously squeezing the light out of my own darkness. But nothing is lost that is worth reclaiming and using. Now my deeper, subtle, unrealistic memories, frustrations, and false guilt complexes have been so weaned away from me that I no longer need or use them to explain reality, society, or myself or to others. Surely, this is the beginning of a new life by a new man in a new ministry. What it finally will be like, I do not know. That bridge can be crossed only when God brings me to it. This is not fatalism on my part, but an honest way of life."

It was within this spirit and setting that I began to travel an un-

115

chartered road toward a normal schedule again. What I had not learned from adults I soon learned through our three children. One creative way was through music. I was never skillful and technically informed in any musical field, but I have loved music all my life. Daily, before I left for the church office, Mary Margaret played my favorite hymns on the piano. It was also a rich challenge to hear little Becky, whose music lessons were less advanced, improve her piano versions of these hymns, too.

Often we sang the hymns and other songs together. We had the times of our lives together—and I sang from the depth of my being, in a bad voice and a musically illiterate fashion. Finally my favorite hymns were reduced to three, and in this order: "A Mighty Fortress Is Our God," "Fairest Lord Jesus," and "O, For a Thousand Tongues to Sing." This was the order of the theology of my new focus and commitment in life, with a sense of a transformed mission as a minister of the Gospel and parent and husband in my own house.

Daily, I went to work with the echo of these songs and the vision of our children's gladness as they played and sang "for Daddy." I did not read devotionals. My hospital experience of letting the Scriptures flow from the depth of my memory and needs was enough for my regular meditation. Sometimes I wondered: "What might have happened if I, like old sick King Saul, had taken time to hear more often 'the music of David.' Or if King Saul had had three little children to play and sing the Christian hymns that we share now? I wonder what would have happened if I had allowed the Word of God to speak to my condition before my breakdown, without biased personal censorship or rationalization?"

Confident that I could handle the pastorate again, I searched my private files in the office. I wanted to make a clean break with two tragic memories and inner conflicts of the period prior to my nervous breakdown. These hoarded communications were symbols of haunting tensions: A secret file of anonymous letters and postal cards threatening my life, reputation, and health; and a collection of offers for professorships from California to Florida, and from the Midwest to the Southwest. I thought: "I'm glad that nobody discovered these things while I was sick. How foolish I was to collect and hide them! I'll destroy them now to bury the past and salute an unknown future. They no longer bother me. After this, I shall no longer be able to dig up these old red flags, if I ever get depressed or too sorry for myself as a preacher."

I destroyed them, glad that I had never shown the written threats to anyone, and few of the many job offers. Reading them over with amusement, I tore up each letter and destroyed the pieces. In doing so, I felt: "I'm making real progress when I can do this with no bitterness or regrets. God is not cruel, but human beings often are. God has His ways of handling false pride. All I need is enough faith and a sense of humor and I can take all such temptations in their stride. I've got to remember how wise Mark Twain was when he observed that human nature is 'fairly well distributed among the human race.'"

This decision lifted a weight from my conscience. In addition, visits to our church services by former Dix Hill associates renewed my courage and will to face reality. From the pulpit, it was a joy to see ex-patients and staff members. This included the frequent presence of Bennie Slaughter from the time of his dismissal as a patient. Certain attendants and nurses whom I had known well dropped by to worship with us. These visitors added to my confidence, for I knew that they believed in me and in my new ministry. Especially was I delighted when Dr. Walter Sikes, the new superintendent of State Hospital, became a member of our congregation on May 1, 1955. I felt that this event was his vote of confidence and perhaps an opening to help, in a small way, to unify our mutual concerns of mental health and religion in greater Raleigh.

In 1955 an entirely new dimension was added to my ministry. This was unplanned and unintentional on my part. As the word leaked out that I was doing some counseling again by January, former mental patients began calling. Relatives and friends of patients also asked for appointments. Accidentally, I had occasional informal chats with troubled people. They stopped me on the streets, in hospitals, and at public gatherings. Always they wanted "to ask just a few questions."

Soon I began to fret too much about such increasing conferences, although I enjoyed them. Therefore Mary casually suggested, "You might wish to read about a famous big-league baseball star who was hospitalized and actually faced a problem much like yours."

"Good," I replied. "Where's the story?"

She pointed out the series of two articles under the title "They Called Me Crazy, and I Was" by Jim Piersall and his collaborator in the *Saturday Evening Post* for late January and early February, 1955. (This was before his book *Fear Strikes Out* followed the articles through.) Eagerly I read the personal story. Then I thought: "This admired Boston Red Sox outfielder has something. He overcame a serious mental illness, and his loss of memory sounds similar to mine. But these things have not kept him from making a complete comeback and being a better ball player than ever. His teammates, opponents, and the entire sports world have reclaimed and accepted him without penalizing him for his mental illness, which seems to have been both similar to and different from mine on the surface. And he did not receive as quick a hospitalization and course of treatments as I did, so perhaps I have some advantage over him there. But his memory lapse involves a longer span than mine."

For weeks, at intervals, I reread Piersall's story. I studied it with self-searching patience. Nothing had so inspired me from current writings. I thought: "Jim Piersall is doing something from his own experience to help other troubled people. He witnesses humbly and gratefully to others, who want the benefit of his encouragement and firsthand encounters, as one who has fully recovered and adjusted to society again."

118

I battled with this challenge for the first six months of 1955. I reviewed my experience prior to my breakdown, realizing that I once had the hope or illusion that I could get well all by myself. "Physician, heal thyself!" was the idea. In those days I had an obsession for counseling beyond my own depths, training, and limits. I had been sleepless over other peoples' problems. For years my counseling with students and parishioners had been normal; but as I grew more conscious of my "successes" in these areas of broken hearts and homes I got the notion that I had a unique knowledge and mastery of this potentially dangerous field. My bookshelves were lined with books and magazines on counseling, mental hygiene, psychotherapy, and religion and psychiatry.

I reflected: "Before my breakdown, my passion for counseling was one of many symptoms of my mental and emotional illness. My library shows that I had a sudden drive toward abnormal study in these fields. This trend is bound to have been symbolic of my own inner hopes that I, by my own readings and self-help, could ward off my own emerging illness." Mary says that I had hinted to her, ahead of the crack-up, that I thought I could get by; but to get me "to a top-flight psychiatrist, who really knows something about the ministry and churches, if I ever do crack up!"

Finally I asked myself: "Am I afraid of the risk of becoming a self-appointed perfectionist again, in a new form now, without knowing it? That I am not an expert in this technical area may not justify my not listening to such troubled people and trying to make suggestions frankly and honestly within my own limits. Jim Piersall is helping troubled people within his limits and in line with his personal background. Perhaps, in my new role of the ministry now, I should give some real time and attention to such people, who ask me to, simply because I am not a technical expert. Suppose I should guide people to reach the proper trained and skilled experts whenever it is obvious that they should be so guided. Perhaps I should encourage those who are experiencing what my own family faced for me, and give some real attention to ex-patients who have not been as fortunate as I in making their readjustments to life and society again. This is a paradox that I must transcend—a bridge that I've got to learn to cross—the problem of being cruel now in my very caution to be kind and from the earnest desire not to risk hurting others by any ignorance and mistakes of my own limited background."

In this spirit, I made my decision: "Okay, just because I do not know *everything* about mental illnesses is no excuse for my doing *nothing* about those plagued with them, if I can be of the least help. I can do the little *something* which I do know. I realize how many of these folks feel, and I know some of the problems they face among their friends, relatives, and even with the specialists. All I have to offer is bits of my own personal story and impressions from my own case. There is no need to make slips and errors which might injure and cause needless suffering among almost helpless people. I realize that I am not a medical doctor nor a psychiatrist, nor am I a substitute for such trained experts. But I can urge people who need such technical help to seek out qualified men and get the best and quickest help possible. And I may help prevent some individuals from being forced to undergo what I did *before it is too late!*"

By summer, 1955, this decision had been worth the battle with my conscience and personal limitations. Myths were spreading about how "Dr. West can help you and advise whether you need professional help or not." This trend was both humbling and annoying. This kind of service was no passion with me, but it was easy, natural, and enjoyable counseling. I found that most disturbed people who sought me out in their struggles with such problems did not expect miracles from me. The details of their problems were often different from mine, but the general problems were remarkably similar. I observed: "Ex-patients usually only want to know if I was ever bothered by readjustment problems like theirs. They all face the same basic fears which I did during my first few months out of State Hospital. They don't expect me to work miracles for them, but to serve as a personal example for them and to share this unique type of fellowship with understanding in our common problems."

I found that ex-patients are most concerned about whether society will always penalize them for having been mentally ill. They want to know if I was disturbed about what "other folks say, especially when they gossip about your having been hospitalized." They want to know if I was ever afraid to face the public again, especially strangers and crowds. They ask, "Do people point you out as one who has been 'insane,' 'crazy,' 'nuts,' or 'off the beam'?" They dislike the unfairness of this outdated popular vocabulary and the odor of such negative labels.

Almost all former patients and concerned observers of them want me to answer these questions: "Do you sleep well now? Do you ever have any severe nervous headaches? Do you ever have any physical pains which the regular medical doctors cannot explain? Do you have nightmares? Do you get restless?" It gives them hope to know that I no longer have headaches, pains, restlessness, or difficulty in sleeping. Most of them are delighted to know of my routine of daily rest.

Such people, as a whole, are not looking for easy answers to their own hard problems. They are trying too desperately to find themselves at ease and at home again in the outside world. They want to talk with someone who had "really come through." They do not want self-pity, but self-respect, confidence, and hope. Most of them have been trying too hard to solve problems that no longer seriously exist, except as they themselves make them. Most of them are trying to cross bridges before they come to them and are not finding peace and joy in a "day-by-day" existence because they try to live either in the distant past or in the remote future.

Former insulin shock patients like to know that I, also, still have the ungodly (or godly) habit of "waking up early" as conditioned by regular treatments for months. They like to know that I detest canned orange juice because of its former associations. And fellow alumni are glad to realize that I believe some nurses are more skilled and gentle in giving needles than others; and that some doctors and specialists are unkind, cruel, and discourteous, whereas others are noble, encouraging, and full of understanding sympathy and suggestions. I usually advise some of them to "go back at times and chat with the ones on the staff whom you really did like and admire as fellow human beings."

When they are too anxious about how society feels or may treat them, I ask: "Do you realize how different it is now from ten years ago? Most people who are in regular hospitals are mentally and emotionally ill. Do you know that millions of Americans have had such illnesses? We are not rare birds or exhibits in society any more. Do you know that the last world war helped our cause? Families all over the nation had relatives or friends who suffered or were hospitalized from 'combat fatigue,' which is just a popular term for a nervous breakdown. So is the term 'nerves.'"

As they begin to realize that the American public is more informed in these realms now than it was a decade ago, they get new hope and confidence. When they note that there are few families who have not had some member or friend who has been hospitalized for mental illness, they begin to trust society more. When they realize that those pathetic persons who look down upon an ex-patient are the ones who deserve pity, and not the former patient, they often feel kinder toward such prejudiced critics.

I never let these ex-patients leave without a challenge to consider what they can do for such ignorance and misunderstanding. They can help. I say, "You can be a good example in adjustment for all returning patients who follow, making it easier upon them." As they see me try to help make people who are awkward and self-conscious in my presence feel at ease, they decide that they will try to do so themselves. We join together in the fraternity of comrades with a mission in the world to help spare others the suffering which we have faced, and to make the future easier for one another.

Often, after such friends leave my office, they welcome outgoing patients of whom they know. They take them out for meals and let them find out for themselves that crowds in restaurants and other public places are not aware of their presence at all. People go to dining places to eat, not to enjoy gossip about those who have been ill.

The realm in which I can be of greatest help to former patients is in understanding. They feel that they know me before they have met me, and I feel that I know them when I see them. Often when they tell me their worries and troubles, I interrupt at some pause to suggest, "You mean, you feel like this. . . ?" They are grateful to have someone else tell them how they feel because they know that I also have felt the same way or I could not describe their own feelings with such feeling myself.

I love and have faith in these former inmates. They know it. I don't get sentimental and tell them so; they sense this love and faith and hope. Sometimes they need understanding which reaches deeper than human speech can go: a nod, a smile and, above all, when they leave, a firm warm handshake or pat on the shoulder or back. "You're doing fine! You're making real progress today! I know that you can make it; if I could, you can"—such words and conveyed thoughts put a new song into their lives and give them a firmer step as they tread toward the outside world.

For a while we have been back in our various hospitals again. We have reviewed our treatments, our progress, and the advice from our experts. We have exchanged jokes and experiences we had behind those locked doors. We have laughed together. We have reviewed our progress toward readjustment together, and we have resolved to be more patient, merciful, and understanding toward society. We have decided that we shall not cross any bridges of decision until we come to them; we shall live a day-by-day existence and "let tomorrow worry about itself." We have shared our families together, and our joy at returning to live again with loved ones and friends.

In such sessions we relive those days when minutes seemed like hours and when days seemed like years. We agree that what we do today is more important than what we did in the past or may do next year. And we share Dr. Proctor's wise advice about loss of memory: "You cannot change the past, can you? Even if you were to remember all that you did in the past. But you can do something about what happens in your life today, can't you? Then let the past be behind us, and do something about the present and the future!" Then what we have forgotten does not seem to us so important after all—not nearly so important as what we learn that we can live by.

11

The Fear of a Relapse

Almost all former patients fear a relapse. I was no exception. Their families and friends fear that they will become ill again under severe stress. Mine was no exception.

Before leaving Dix Hill, I became aware of this problem. Numbers of patients were "serving" their second and third "terms." A veteran of many readmittances told me: "When you get out of here, remember what I say. Remember it all your life. I believe a guy like you can beat the game. I never will, myself."

"What should I remember?" I asked.

"This," he said. "It isn't the strangers and folks who won't trust you because they heard you were put away once while you were off your rocker; they don't hurt you the worst. They only gossip and pester you and spread their ideas and lies as to why you went crazy. Some gossips think they have inside dope that you are still crazy. They can worry you and cause your guts to dry up inside you if you're stupid enough to let them. Take me, I can handle such folks myself. I feel sorry for them, because I know they haven't got the sense or the guts I've got. I don't pay them no mind at all!"

"Yes," I agreed, "I see your point. I don't believe folks who distrust or fear me will ever trouble my spirit again either. But who tempts you to betray yourself from the inside?"

Sadly, he answered, "*It's your own best friends and relatives that you've got to watch!* They're fatal, because you really love them and they really love you. If they won't believe in you enough to let you fight your own battles inside, if they won't give you the chance to test your own metal, your own guts, your own faith in yourself— why, when the chips are down you feel sorry for them. And you get to hating yourself for causing them so much worry over you, 'til you hate that you were ever born in the first place! Then, I warn you, you'll get bitter at yourself. When you can't stand yourself any longer as the weak and black sheep of your own family and friends, you get bitter at those that love you the most, and your goose is cooked. You can't see straight, can't think straight, and you can't tell your enemies from your friends. It isn't that you hate them or yourself at first, but you hate what the head-doctors call 'their domination.' They don't mean to sell you short. They just can't help it. They figure that because they love you, they own you. They won't even let you learn to housebreak yourself with the public!"

Shaking my hands, he implored: "Remember, Preacher, you must set an example for a lot of people when you get out. Please help keep other guys like me from ever coming back to this here insane asylum! When the going gets toughest, remember me, will you? Hold your head high and keep your heart big and be kind to those who aren't able to stand or understand us patients. Look everybody in the eye and love them like you loved us sick folks here. And you let them know that you are from Dix Hill, and proud of it, Preacher! You aren't ashamed of it now; don't you ever get ashamed of it then. There wouldn't be any Dix Hills if the public would understand us folks and themselves at the same time. We might get crazy, but the outside world hasn't got any sense about us yet. Preacher, don't talk about love; just live it. Maybe that's the only way the public will ever learn to know what we need—the kind of love that hasn't got any strings attached. And don't talk about religion, either; just live it. I don't want any part of the churches' re-

ligion in the outside world. It's not for a guy like me; but I need the
kind you show."

I remarked, "But you seem so happy here now. Why?"

He said: "I'll be a lifelong patient here, I guess—off and on, that
is. I can't hold up to what I know when I get out each time!
Preacher, I wish you knew the home folks in my small town. You'd
understand as nobody could. But don't you be sorry for me. Remember, I'm not exactly useless, myself. It helps me to tell folks
like yourself, and warn them to remember my fix when they go back
to the outside world. I bet I keep some ex-patients from going crazy
again better than these here head-doctors who have never been sick
themselves. They tell us only what they learn from books and
studies. Sure, they study us patients, too—I want to be fair to 'em—
but they haven't learned to study themselves enough first. Not many
of them understand how us patients feel and think—but they all
think they do!"

Perhaps the veteran saved my life. Little did I suspect then that
I would be led by his advice about friends and relatives so often.
The crucial tests came when least expected, but not until the spring
and summer of 1955.

Long before these crises, I had learned to fear and respect the
love of my closest kin and friends without letting them know it.
Early I took in stride the usual bombardment of questions: "You
look fine, Fred. But are you sure you feel as well as you look? Aren't
you overdoing again?"

I told myself: "Thanks to my friend at Dix Hill, I don't resent
these overanxious and protective concerns. I'm grateful for their
love and interest, but my own deep happiness, joy, and peace of
mind are beyond their experience and knowledge to sense. I can see
why my health seems too good to them to seem real or to last. I
won't try to explain to them, lest they think I'm on the defensive.
Or, worse, I might hurt their feelings."

However, at times I could not refrain from teasing them, saying:

127

"I never felt better. What did you expect? What did you come out to see, a reed shaken by the wind? Why are you surprised that I am so stable?" But I made these remarks gently, and with affection for those who were unduly apprehensive, yet honest and sincere.

My family and relatives did not so test me. I thought: "They have complete confidence in me. They give me full freedom to face my own personal problems and decisions. But it may be possible for my close friends, who love me the most, to hurt me in their very efforts to be kind and good. Suppose they eventually shake my family's trust in me? What if they accidentally probe the most sensitive spots? What if they innocently twist signs of profound health so that they appear to be old, recurring symptoms of illness?" Particularly, I dreaded this in regard to my increasing counseling with the mentally ill and their kin. Thus for months I was afraid that I would be robbed of a unique joy of my new ministry. Deeply I craved the chance to be my genuine self. At times I was tempted to fake more worries and tiredness than I had in order to appease my friends' too aggressive love and anxiety. But I decided that that would be a cheap effort to escape facing reality and life as society lives it.

Before these trends died, I faced a crisis in early 1955. I knew it could bring a relapse—or even deeper stability. This problem unfolded through a series of anonymous telephone calls, letters, and messages—not from friends, but from a few who hated me and feared that I would not crack up again. My relatives and friends did not find out about this systematic series of threats and advice until I had written this book.

A flood of calls and messages came day and night for weeks. Well timed, they interrupted me during every serious undertaking. The monotony and repetition of the disturbed voices of these bitter folks reminded me vividly of the "strange voices" I had heard when I was emerging from my blackout at State Hospital.

Someone would say: "You haven't got well yet, have you? Why

be so stubborn? Wise up! You are only ruining your health and church again. You are only causing Mr. White and Mr. Ellis to suffer for you. We'd hate to have to break all three of you down!" Then the telephone receiver on the other end of the line would be hung up with a loud metallic click.

Another voice would yell roughly: "If you stay here, you'll split our church wide open! Who wants a minister with the reputation of splitting churches? A second crack-up will end you. Dr. West, you were a good college professor. Go back into education, or you'll soon go back to an insane asylum. Take your choice." Then the person would hang up.

Another stratagem followed: "Quit trying to make stooges out of your church leaders. Why be a dictator when you can't handle your own spirit?" Later, such calls as this came: "Getting sick again, aren't you? Your last lousy sermon proves it. Another sermon like that famous one of 1953 is just around the corner; then you'll be put away forever. Why commit suicide? Wise up. I'm really one of your best friends and admirers. But you're too sick to realize it now."

These encounters did not hurt my feelings. They renewed my faith. Often they sent me to prayer. Usually I prayed: "O God, You have been so real and near me in times and conditions tougher than these. Be my good and merciful Shepherd yet, lest I forget. I need You so. Only Your love and understanding can satisfy my deepest cravings. Keep my soul calm, my mind clear; and help me to say and do the right thing for Your Kingdom through Your living and loving Word. Forgive me for not being able to love these enemies yet as I believe that Jesus would have me love them. I confess that I have not learned to respect them, but only to pity them. I know that their suffering is too deep for me to understand—too dangerous for me to risk trying to do only what Christ can do for them. I am all too human; I need You and Your love, and they do, too. O God, help me ever to remember that they are Your children, not mine; and that I am not their Judge and Redeemer, but You are. If I am too weak to love them and help them as You can, if it be Your holy Will, help me always to be kind to them and never to get mad and fight back as they want me to do."

At times, I did kindly thank the telephone caller for his advice and concern before he could hang up his receiver. I destroyed the secret written messages without revealing their arrival to anyone. Whenever I feared that I might rebel against the incessant monotony of these approaches, I prayed: "O God, forgive them and me. We have all sinned. Make me 'as wise as a serpent and as harmless as a dove.'" But I never fought back or protested.

I decided: "Perhaps these temptations are good for me. In the long run, they will separate the men from the boys. I shall not play these childish games; I shall treat all such persons as adults if and when they come into the open. These events remind me that, at best, I can never be perfect and sinless in the Kingdom of God; and at worst my new maturity, like my old beastliness, is only skin deep." Constantly I thanked God for the veteran patient's advice, hearing the echo and challenge of his words: *Remember, I'm not exactly useless, myself.* I knew that I owed much to that strange Ezekiel in the watchtower on Dix Hill.

Soon a public crisis arose. A "Forty Years of Hillyer Memorial" suddenly appeared in attractive booklet form. It was carefully distributed among our members, and circulated among religious leaders throughout the state and beyond. This history covered the story of our local church from its origin to its alleged fortieth anniversary celebration in 1955. The Foreword implied that the author was asked to do the job at the request of our Official Board, but claimed that the booklet was "a project" of one of our men's groups. The publication contained pictures of every minister in the history of our congregation with the exception of myself. Summaries of the employment and fine contributions of all the other ministers were included, together with their dates of tenure. Although neither my name nor my ministry in our church was mentioned, events were reported which involved our church family during my pastorate.

Both my wife and I were amused. The booklet did not irk us, nor did we resent its author or his helpers. But our members and lay leaders did not accept the account so lightly, nor did a number of ministers of other denominations in Raleigh, or key Disciples ministers in and beyond the state. But Mary and I refused to comment or criticize. We did not object to Raleigh's newspaper announcements of the publication.

A noted churchman suggested: "Why don't you send a copy to the Disciples of Christ Historical Society for its permanent records? This booklet might make invaluable research material someday!"

Many of my friends feared that the publication would cause me to have another nervous breakdown. They felt that I would not be able to stand the pressure of the inevitable heated reactions. Our Official Board refused to ignore the booklet, being concerned for the good name and reputation of our church. Most of them assumed that the booklet was a slap in the face at our leaders as well as a "subtle" attack on me. Furthermore, they felt that the booklet and its attendant newspaper publicity would give the public the false impression that the publication was published with the knowledge and sanction of the Official Board. Actually, no fortieth-anniversary celebration of the church had ever been scheduled, and no such event had occurred such as was implied in the press and by the Foreword. Some men were distressed that their names had been used to sanction the booklet without their knowledge or consent.

As a result, our Official Board passed a motion to "officially disapprove" the "Forty Years of Hillyer Memorial," and to so inform our membership and the author in writing. The resolution was published in Raleigh's press, and was sent to some key religious leaders throughout the state and nation. To my knowledge, no one desired any revenge involving the author or his silent helpers. Although many resented the booklet, they understood the human beings who had made it possible. They were treated, not as "enemies" but as "persons." The issues were based upon Christian ethics and truth, not personalities. I took no part in the discussions, making no personal or public stand, one way or another.

As a result, I told Mary: "Enough leaders are now ready to stand up for their own faith and convictions, whether it makes them popular with the little handful, or 'Old Guard' faction—which dominated this church and its ministers for decades—or not. Our leaders have learned—the hard way—not to follow the line of least resistance. They want the truth known through the spirit of love and good will. Soon our Board will ignore the individuals—or outvote them—who want to have this church and its growing Christian program run by those who get the maddest, yell the loudest, and pray the most acceptable public prayers, only to be seen and heard of men. I believe that our how-to-win-friends-and-influence-people era of 'rule or ruin' is almost over. I pity those who refuse to learn Milton's insight in *Paradise Lost* about the fallen spirit who would rather 'reign in hell than serve in heaven.' I'll set an example for them, if they'll let me."

But I was too optimistic. The tensions did not decline, but increased. I had yet to battle for my inner life in other unexpected public crises. Just when I had proudly assumed that the gates of Hell and its hate could not budge me again, I was brought to temporary despair.

The most heartbreaking test was over within a few hours. However, as I had learned in the hospitals, a brief interval can seem like forever when one is under severe pressure. I was heatedly attacked at a Board meeting. A sermon was taken to pieces and interpreted without accurate quotation or understanding of its spirit or content. In doing so, the Old Guard leader pictured me as a "troublemaker behind all the hard feelings and bitterness" engulfing "our whole church." He charged that previous pastors had "poured oil upon our wounds" to heal differences, but that I had only added "gasoline to the flames" and had "deliberately fanned the flames" in order to "boss" the whole church and its leadership.

Praying silently during the entire episode, I sensed the suffering of the vast majority of the Board present. Only one person responded from the floor—a lady, a deaconess. She insisted that the opposite type of sermon had been preached by me than was being reported; then she gave a better summary of the sermon than I could have given. In tears, she left the room. A motion to adjourn was passed quickly.

Quietly, I went to my office alone. No one said a word to me. Soon the chairman of the Board appeared, refusing to let anyone else in. How well he knew me and understood! He never said a word, letting me cry my heart out. I was not touched by self-pity, but I was hurt, bitter, and angry. Suddenly all my hopes, dreams, and prayers for a genuine Christian transformation of our church had been crushed. Sadly, and with tears in his eyes, Mr. H. Glenn White gave me freedom to be myself privately, even at my worst. Then he put an arm around me, saying nothing, until I felt that his was God's arm.

Finally, I assured him not to worry about me. "I can make it," I said. "But I need a little time. I want to go out now and drink a lot of coffee and do some thinking alone. I don't want Mary to see me this low when I go home."

He trusted me, and let me go. But some intimate friends joined me at their own insistence and from obvious compassion. At the coffee shop, I could not control my tongue or temper. As I had long feared, I turned upon my friends bitterly. I said: "Don't think that that man can hurt me any more. It's not he but my friends, whom I can't admire now as Christian leaders. Sure, I was mad at him at the office. But I was wrong. Now I see him differently. He's the smartest local church politician I ever saw, with real guts as well as brass. He's got more brains and guts than all our peace-at-any-price Board has put together, including you! It took a woman—a widow with all her mite—to give any response to his charges. That's the trouble with our church lay leadership and with me: I used to speak when I should have been silent. Now I must be silent under such personal attacks and criticism while our lay leaders have neither the guts nor the faith to share openly what they confide to me privately."

Wisely, they let me talk myself out of my bitter despair. They did not lecture or advise me too much. When I calmed down, I went home. Mary encouraged me to talk it all over with her. When I went to bed, I slept in peace, understanding myself and my own weaknesses and impatience better. Before dozing off, I asked God's "forgiveness and mercy to teach me a lesson from this brief, possibly abnormal, tendency."

Ultimately, that one tendency toward bitterness was a healthy, if not saving, personal defeat. From the next morning on, I was only grateful for the new lesson I had learned about myself.

But by the middle of May, 1955, I found myself escaping the church tensions in an emergency. With only one night's warning, I was on a plane to St. Petersburg, Florida. I was sure that no more personal attacks by my critics could come close to cracking me again. But I was convinced that I had to get away from the over-anxiety and fears of my best friends. I did not want to risk possible resentment against my supporters who could not accept my honest version as to how well I really did feel.

During the trip I was happy. I felt: "Here I am running away from Raleigh in order to survive. But this time it is no flight from reality, but to reality. How odd it is that I am not running away from my critics, but from those who love me the most!"

I thought: "Friends put my wife under unnecessary pressures to hasten my annual month's vacation by two weeks. They coaxed even her to urge me to take this trip with no advance notice to the congregation. I could tell at the airport that Mary was not nearly so upset as our friends were. Had I stayed, they might continue long enough to shake her confidence in me or make it too rugged for her by their visits and earnest advice. This trip will give Mary the freedom she needs. These friends are reading their own personal struggles and sufferings into mine. Perhaps this flight will be best for all of us."

I roomed for a week with my brother George, who was giving some addresses at our state convention in St. Petersburg. Then George and I went to Pass-A-Grille to fish together. We hired a guide to show us the best places to catch trout. He taught us how to use a spinner rod and reel. Whenever we erred, he cursed a blue streak. After one eloquent outburst, he roared with laughter. He explained: "You guys want to hear something funny? Last week I took a gent out. When he lost a fish, I cussed my head off like I've done all my life. Fishing and cussing is all I've known. My dad and his dad were professional fishermen, too. I was raised that way. But this guy cuts in and says: 'Sir, I demand that you refrain from profanity and vulgar language. The very idea of taking the Lord's name in vain! I'll have you know that I am a well known minister of the Gospel in St. Petersburg!' "

We all laughed gleefully. The fisherman snorted: "What a jackass I was! Usually I can smell a damn' preacher anywhere. But this guy don't look the type. He acted like a human being until I cussed. Why are all preachers such pious jokers? Why can't they understand an ordinary fisherman and his language?"

Glancing at George, I replied: "I'd like to know too! Some preachers you can spot a mile. Others you wouldn't know if they were sitting right next to you, like we are. Isn't that so, George?" After that, every time George and I looked at each other, we grinned.

As we fished, I kept thinking: "If you only knew, my friend! Our Lord Himself did a good job with a few rugged fishermen. The Galilean Carpenter does understand fishermen and preachers alike. But I'll bet we preachers today give His world-wide mission and message a bigger handicap and more superficial appeal than all the fishermen and their traditions in the world. Profanity cannot hurt the Church where it counts in human lives, but we preachers can when we try to reduce Jesus Christ and His way of life to our own size. Fred, you must learn to make the Bible more real and helpful to people like this guide; the Church needs the Peter, James, John, and Andrew fishing folk of our day. I admire honest skeptics more than I do secondhand and second-rate believers in mediocre Christian faith and life, which have so little vitality and love."

When public school was out, Mary and the children spent two happy weeks with me on the Gulf Coast. We did not even discuss the Raleigh church situation.

Suddenly a new crisis arose. Before the full month's vacation ended, an intimate friend and key leader of the church telephoned. He urged me to rush back with my family to preach on Sunday and to attend that night's Board meeting. He insisted: "Don't ask me why. Don't worry about a thing. Just trust your Board. We know what we are doing. To help us, all you have to do is to show up, preach, and be your own genuine self. Please do this for the church's sake and for your own. Everything will come out okay."

When we returned, the members and leaders seemed very glad to see me. At the Board meeting, which was remarkably peaceful, I thought: "Some underground game must be going on again. But most of the Board members appear unusually confident and happy, except for the few who look as if they have received a death sentence."

Later, I found out why. I had been sitting on a powder keg, not realizing it. I was told: "Fred, while you were on vacation, we didn't want to bother you with our problems, which we knew we had to face ourselves. You see, the rumor was planted that we had spirited you away to a mental institution in Florida for another nervous breakdown. The story was that Mary and the church leaders had lied to our congregation. Isn't that incredible?"

I felt sorry for the small minority of our leaders who had become so desperate.

The plan had been to pass, while I was away, a resolution to discharge me from my office. But my appearance at the meeting had foiled their strategy. Such a motion, if it had been passed by the misinformed Board, could not have won the needed majority vote of the congregation. But it could have caused confusion, especially among intimate friends, as to whether or not Mary and I could survive such tactics. Moreover, the news of my alleged "second nervous breakdown" had already reached students and churchmen in other sections of the nation, and even overseas in the Holy Land. My tennis friends throughout the state were also upset for a while by the "confidential story."

After this experience, every former fear of any possible relapse on my part vanished, never to return. When my friends found out that the plot did not irk or upset me, their fears of my becoming ill again under church pressures disappeared, too. Then, for the first time, I understood better why so many of our members and lay leaders had kept saying, "Give people enough rope, and they'll hang themselves."

I decided: "This applies to me as well as to my critics. To get rid of my fear of a possible relapse, I had to be given enough rope to have my faith and spirit fully tested on my own. And that may be what all my friends needed for themselves, too—enough leeway to prove their own growing vital Christian faith at its depths."

The myth of my relapse was the acid test for our lay leaders and congregation. After that, a profound spirit of mutual trust and Christian community emerged with unique vitality and power. The final showdown concerning the future program and leadership of our church was an anticlimax. When the Old Guard could not regain enough voting power to elect its own set of officers to the Official Board, a church split was inevitable. But the split gave both the opposing minority and the vast majority of members the freedom to express and share their ways of religious life with freedom and without controversy.

I knew now that the Lord had become the Shepherd of a mighty group of people through an unconquerable spirit and leadership among our congregation. We all owed much of this inner victory, peace, and vitality to the veteran patient on Dix Hill who had said, "Remember, I'm not exactly useless, myself."

12

When Relatives and Friends Are Kind

Concerned relatives and friends of patients or potential patients ask, "What can we do?" Often they suffer as much as the ones who are mentally ill. But the suffering of these kin and friends is different. Too few know what such patients experience: how they feel when they are confined or how they will react when they do return to the outside world. Too many relatives are as worried as the patients about the possible effect on their own status in outside society, once rumors reach the public that their loved ones are hospitalized.

I spend more time with relatives and close friends of patients than with those who are, or have been, ill. Relatives and friends play vital roles in the recovery and progress of patients who are on the road back to reality and who are learning to face themselves more realistically. Close loved ones always play crucial roles in the readjustments of patients to home life and to normal society.

Most such troubled people ask, "What did your folks do to help you?" From my own limited insights and personal experience implied or described in the previous chapters, I tell them my story. I describe the letters and visits of my kin and friends. I suggest: "When you are homesick, a sample of home is the only thing to cure it. There is no substitute for the human family and friends who have meant so much in a patient's life. There are things that relatives and friends can do for patients which no trained staff and technical experts can possibly do or replace. Nothing takes the place of the tender comradeship of one's own family and friends outside the hospital. In these realms, if I were you, I would get advice from the staff as to the problems and needs of the individual patient, and how best to approach him."

Often I say: "To give you some idea of what you can do, here is what I saw. Whenever I got homemade cookies, cakes, and even gifts like cigarettes from my relatives or friends, my sick wardmates were delighted to share them—not because they were so hungry or too poor to buy cigarettes, but because they said these things came from some patient's home, family, or friends. In some cases, families and friends were almost inhuman, and certainly unkind, in not taking the time to write regularly. There is far more value to such a letter or card than the time it takes to write it or the postage required to send it. Merely giving of your time to a patient means much to him. When patients are able to read, they desire news from home and from old friends. Some patients were sent money, but no news from home. We had little use for money behind those walls. But some of my comrades were bankrupt for the most priceless of all human gifts—kindness, mercy, understanding, and hope from home. As much as anything else, I always wanted to know that my folks were getting along all right, and that they were not worried or fearful of what would happen to me. Their letters and visits did the job. They shared only enough news about themselves and the family to make me want more, but they never left me apprehensive about them. Correspondence and personal gifts from home mean much, but they are no substitutes for personal visits when the staff is sure that a patient is ready and needs the visits."

Whatever else I share with relatives and friends of patients, I always stress that their kindness is needed. I add: "When you do not know what to do or say, you can always be kind. You can try to put yourself in the sick patient's place. To me, kindness heals and reveals. It is a result of unselfish love and good will. Such kindness is next to personal understanding, which is often its fruit."

When patients are ready to return to the outside world, I urge those near and dear to share with the hospital staff every possible question and doubt as to what they can do to help the approaching readjustments. Some hospitals teach the family to understand its unique role in a person's reorientation to society. But some hospitals and key staff members simply do not get this job done. If this were not so, I wouldn't have so many anxious people coming to me. If they were helped and guided as effectively as we were at Graylyn, their ranks would be fewer. On the other hand, some specialists do adequate jobs professionally, but suggest to certain people that they drop by and have a chat with me. Perhaps this is mostly because some need a personal story and suggestions from one who has seen, from the inside, what a patient's mysterious and complex world looks like. Other disturbed relatives and friends merely want my assurance to confirm what technical advisers have already more ably shared with them, while craving more practical hints or helps.

However, specialists sometimes muddy the waters in dealing with patients' relatives and friends. Some seem to take pleasure in "telling relatives off," lacking good manners as well as sympathy and kindness. Some, who may be able in research or treatments, are poor in counseling. They tend to "bawl out" patients and relatives, "preaching at them" as though they want to arouse their fears and deepen their shame. Such people have suffered enough, often from false guilt complexes; they need patient and sympathetic advice. I give time to such victims because I finally discovered how my wife felt when she was rudely and incompetently treated by some officials and staff who were in positions of power and authority but who were immature human beings in their own professions. When persons like that are discussed with me, I usually suggest: "How about going to the chaplain or to some able psychiatrist such as I can name? You have no quarrel with any of the staff; what you want now is to help get the patient on his feet again. Isn't that right?"

A great many personal problems usually baffle relatives and friends. Especially, they ask: "Should we keep it secret or confidential that So-and-So has been mentally and emotionally ill? Should we try to get the patient another job when he returns? Wouldn't it be easier if our whole family moved to another state where the patient will not be penalized by people who are afraid to trust him or let him return to his old job? Shouldn't the children be 'protected' from the knowledge that their father, mother, sister, or brother has been ill and 'put away'?"

I reply, "These are tough problems, and there are no easy answers." I remind such people that I am no expert, and certainly not the Lord speaking. In some cases, I know that individuals are handicapped by the embarrassment of relatives, particularly in small communities and among small-minded people who offer little understanding or help. I stress: "I am convinced that modern society, in most cases, rejoices in the healthy return of patients and gives them a fair opportunity to prove themselves again. In our kind of mobile culture, the situation is rare wherein the news can be ultimately censored. From what I have seen of many ministers who are ex-patients, I am convinced that it is better to face life frankly, honestly, and openly than to live in pretense, false shame, and loneliness." However, I always suggest this much: "It is healthier to tell a minimum of truth to sympathetic and understanding friends than later to run the risk of shock that might block needed help by others through distorted gossip and whispers of self-appointed angels and devils.

"The truth makes us free. Otherwise we become slaves to the least informed, the most prejudiced and inhuman forces in some communities. In many cases, up-to-date family doctors, ministers, and professional and business leaders deserve to know the truth about patients in order to be of the greatest help in their own way

—both openly and behind the scenes. Influential leaders and civic-minded people often can smooth the rough road of readjustment for ex-patients and their families. The family, in turn, needs to trust society and its most able servants; it is good for humane leaders of both community and family life to trust and to be trusted. When we ourselves fail to trust people, we do not give them a chance to trust us and to champion an inspiring cause such as ours, which is world-wide, and not merely local or provincial, in scope."

Close relatives and friends can help a patient whose memory has been lost or confused. Such loss of memory usually embraces short periods of time—weeks or months, ordinarily. Those close to a recovering patient can tactfully help him to "save face" and to avoid unnecessary embarrassment when he fumbles for words and does not know how to respond to questions and remarks concerning which his memory is blank. My wife has done this so well that friends with whom I had traveled, persons whom I had newly met, and even those whom I had married do not know that I fail to recall such events in the months prior to my breakdown.

We would not have minded telling the full truth. I was not embarrassed, but I did dislike to embarrass innocent acquaintances who mentioned things which meant much to them. In fact, I do not mind when someone knows that I know nothing of which he speaks so long as it does not hurt his feelings or cause him to "lose face." Sometimes people talk so fast and commit themselves so completely about certain events involving me that they feel badly when they are informed that I don't know what they're talking about. Basically, they are my personal problems and my kin's, not problems of other people whose memories of events in their lives are dear to them. Whenever possible, my wife "briefs" me and coaches me ahead of time. This filled-in memory is as much of an inspiration to me as an original recollection. I gladly trust, and must trust, the reporting of those who understand my limitations.

Perhaps the worst problem in this realm of lost and confused memory is that too many psychiatrists and hospitals, using deep shock treatments and "miracle drugs" with similar effects, do not prepare either the patients or their close kin for what they can expect or for their response to these normal reactions to various therapies. Sometimes the patients are prepared, but forget the advance warnings. But close relatives often need such preparations even more than do most patients. Relatives can do more about such situations when they do occur, whereas former patients are likely to be frustrated.

Some psychiatrists, because they do not have the staff or facilities for hospitalization, treat only those who are mildly and superficially mentally and emotionally ill. They are able in their trade and skill. But a few others seem too desirous of easy money, and offer simple solutions to deeply complex problems. For example, some tend to give electric shock treatments to every patient, regardless of his needs and conditions—like the outmoded general practitioner who still gives aspirin to a person with fever, sinus trouble, itch, or a contagious disease. Usually such specialists brief neither the patients nor their relatives adequately for possible lapses of memory.

Troubled people come to me after going to second- and third-rate specialists who, as described by one practitioner, are "filling-station psychiatrists." Some patients are too profoundly ill to recover from mere physical treatments or drugs alone. They need competent care and guidance in a well equipped hospital. To such persons and their relatives, I suggest that they consult the best psychiatrists for more profound help and care. I explain: "There are ministers and ministers, doctors and doctors, lawyers and lawyers, and psychiatrists and psychiatrists, but they are not all of equal ability and understanding in their own vocations. Though their academic degrees and training are standard, they may still be mediocre performers, at best. The same is true of many teachers and professors, farmers and salesmen, housewives and fishermen. The parable of Jesus about those

144

with five and three talents, and one talent, respectively, is relevant to human gifts and abilities."

When illnesses are not in advanced stages, I often recommend some specialists who are not top experts. But I urge such patients to ask questions and get all the advice they can, before and after treatments. When it is obvious that patients are profoundly ill, I urge them to go to the best specialists at once. And I do not hesitate to tell them: "Professional ethics or no professional ethics, it is a matter of personal experience and Christian ethics to me. One trouble with most inexperienced families in this realm is the modern fad that 'a psychiatrist is all you need'! But who and what he is, and the results he is known to achieve, are as important as his professional title and degree."

However, the biggest problem is not the psychiatrists. Most of them know their limits, although some are not self-critical of their personal ethics and limitations. The major problem is the dangerous trend among medical doctors whose professional training was completed long ago and who have not kept up with recent progress in treating mental and emotional illnesses. They may even deal with a patient who is already planning to commit murder or suicide, and overlook the signs that are obvious even to relatives or to former patients.

Such doctors often hate, despise, and fear psychiatry and mental institutions—as too many out-of-date clergymen do! Some know their own limitations, but won't face them. They observe only the superficial trends which they want to believe and follow, but ignore the fact that they are trying to treat and manipulate persons beyond the scope of their own depths and skills. These doctors use "miracle drugs" to "cure" profoundly ill people who are ultimately helpless without the aid of first-rate psychiatrists. Nor do the suicides of their depressed patients—further depressed by the drugs such doctors have prescribed—seem to improve either their professional ethics or their understanding that they are playing with bundles of human dynamite beyond their own understanding and training.

Untold numbers of people confide in me that they are using "happy pills," or tranquilizers, and new miracle drugs on doctors' orders, but wonder why they keep getting worse after a few weeks of temporary relief. Others wonder why their memories fade and become confused. Many tell me that they get their "mental drugs" from nonmedical friends and nonprofessional advisers. I saw one such person stagger down the aisle of my church, as a matron of honor at a wedding, as though drunk. Afterwards she explained that she had "borrowed a couple of pills for a quick pick-up for nerves" before the wedding.

Few of these people ask me for appointments, although many are disturbed by a terrible sense of shame and guilt, and say, "Something is wrong with me because the doctor said my pills should have made me well months ago." They stop me in public places to ask, "Do you take these medicines?" They seem surprised and disappointed that I do not, and wonder why I sleep well and never have any more "nervous headaches."

I am among those who believe that all of us should worry, or feel anxiety, insecurity, unhappiness, restlessness, and fear, within normal limits. Such feelings are as normal as laughter, prayer, conversation, and recreation for normal people. They are signs of real moral, spiritual, and psychological health. I agree with those specialists who now warn that a person may be mentally and emotionally sick if he does not do some worrying, and have some disturbing fears, doubts, and senses of guilt. This problem involves the thin line between normal feelings and abnormal feelings about normally complex problems and difficult decisions. The line between love and hate is thin. The line between a sick bitterness and a healthy disgust is thin. So is the difference between a saint and a spiritual snob at the dividing line. The line between a mental hospital and the outside world is often thinner than the walls which separate the two.

Who prescribes the use of the great new drugs, and with what skill and counsel, is all-important.

Another group of people includes those who know that their loved ones are seriously ill. Doctors, ministers, and families have not been able to coax the potential patients to get voluntary help. They sadly inquire, "What can we relatives and close friends do?"

I counter with questions like these: "Do you really want your husband (or son or friend) to get well? How much do you love him? How intelligently do you want to love him? Do you think that you are being kind to him to let him risk his life or yours? Are you being just to society? Are you being merciful when you do not have him taken involuntarily for confinement and help? Or are you mainly thinking of your own pride and how the loved one may react to you personally for a temporary period? Can you get an up-to-date medical doctor to help you to have the patient committed—whether he wants to go or not—if all love and advice have failed?"

When they ask me if they will ever be "forgiven" by the loved ones for involuntary commitments, I reply: "I was taken against my knowledge and consent. I resented my loved ones' doing so. Now I thank God that they were so kind and merciful to me. What do you think that your responsibility and love require?"

Most relatives are kind, when they love their kin enough to descend into Hell with them, or to take them to its gates, in order that they may know how close Heaven is to God's earth and people.

With relatives who care and share, I like to discuss a favorite proverb. It is an old saying with new truth for those who face severe anxiety, fear, insecurity, illness, loneliness, sorrow, and disturbing distress. This proverb of crisis declares that such persons "will either deepen or they will splinter." This is true both of patients and of their relatives who suffer in sharing their sufferings. Out of such crises can come bigger and better people than ever before, or tragedy beyond imagination.

This is a universal problem. It is spun out of the vast web of human tension. Potentially, it includes every person's struggle to erase or to retrace the image of God within him. To me, this proverb makes vivid man's tragedy and his dignity for God's glory and everybody's well-being.

Frequently, relatives tell me, "We are afraid that we, too, may go to pieces under the pressures of strain and stress while our loved one is hospitalized." With them I often discuss another proverb: "When it gets dark enough, you can see the stars." Then I add: "Your loved one will come out of this experience well, with your help and understanding, and both you and he will see a splendor and glory in life that might not have been possible had not these clouds come at this time."

I assure them that this is the story of untold numbers of us who have fallen beneath life's dark shadows to live in a grim, hostile world without meaning and color. "But," I emphasize, "we have been led back again to see the same world that you see—and to see ourselves and others in a more healthy light and focus than ever before. We are among the many today who have had critical 'nervous breakdowns,' 'crack-ups,' 'combat fatigues'—mental and emotional illnesses. We had to become extremely childish and helpless until we were prepared by specialists and kind relatives and friends to receive greater maturity and confidence.

"So, you see, what you do for and with your loved ones under such pressures is extremely important. But what you are—and especially how you react to these pressures yourselves—is vital to them. This is really a matter of how deeply and unselfishly you do love them, and of how kind you wish to be to them for their own happiness in the long run."

13

God Is Not Cruel

Distressed people visit me as a minister because their faith in God is being tested. The faith of vast numbers is wavering. In others, a new, vital faith is being born. Emerging from an unexpected depth, the problem, at first, frightens them. Some are afraid of a cruel and fickle man-made deity of their own or of an immature society's fancy. I listen carefully, with sympathy, to all such people. In so doing I confess: "I know how you feel. I once felt much the same way myself." Mental and emotional illness is not necessarily their primary problem, but a symptom of a spiritual "sickness unto death"—to borrow a phrase from Sören Kirkegaard, whose personal life and writings have become intensely vital to me since my breakdown and recovery.

Not all who come to me are mentally ill, but many are potential candidates. They are victims of a morally and spiritually sick culture. And they share a pathetic interpretation of diseases among those they love or hate, accept or resent. Such persons tend to be morally and spiritually sick and lonely in their own souls. Their problems are normal in certain levels of society and among intolerant movements which worship and proclaim a harsh and cruel God. Such a God does not say to them through an Isaiah, "Come, and let us reason together, saith the Lord." Such a God is devoid of reason, goodness, forgiveness, and mercy. These people have been led to believe that the Lord God of all history and mankind is no one's Good Shepherd, but everyone's immature dictator and tyrant. They know God only as an unjust and petty Judge who demands his pound of flesh at any price or any individual's ruin, driving them to shun the one true God in utter frustration, fear, and despair.

But such people do not experience the real, living God of the Hebrew-Christian faith as the only actual Creator, Judge, and Redeemer of all mankind, including themselves. It is no accident that both the Church and the Synagogue, as well as the Bible, proclaim God in threefold terms—whether by creed or by action—as our holy, universal Creator, Judge, and Redeemer. This healthy religious faith can multiply human understanding and unselfish love, as well as a devout sense of community and communication devoted uniquely to the highest and best that are in the hidden depths of all human beings. This God of reality ever speaks to our essential nature and condition through every human situation and event.

Lesser views of God are too human, finite, or inhuman for normal healthy life. Frequently they lead to abnormal reactions or to sterile faith on the part of believers. When people hazard these moods, I share my basic new faith: "God loves everybody on the face of His earth. He loves us all, no matter what may happen to us or to our loved ones at times. God is a Shepherd who sends His holy Son to live and die for His sheep—to prod them with His rod and staff, and to lead them tenderly to greener pastures and less turbulent waters. This God-in-Christ identifies himself with all suffering humanity. He comes 'not to condemn, but to save the whole world.' If you think of God as obviously cruel or as a subtle barbarian Destroyer and Preserver—and not as the ground of all being, existence, love, light, truth, and spirit—my friend, you need to learn what these sacred Biblical beliefs and trusts can mean and imply for your life. Your battle is not with God, but between your own faith and soul."

Such disturbed people often ask me, "How could God allow such an illness to happen to anyone, especially to someone as good as my boy?"

In answer, I like to quote Dr. Ralph Sockman's insight that "war is not God's will, but God's agony." And I share my personal faith in a more than personal God, who impersonally allows mental and emotional illnesses, as well as wars, to rain down upon the just and the unjust, upon the pious and the irreverent, upon the rich and the poor, upon both the educated and the uneducated, and, yes, upon clergymen and laymen alike.

I explain: "This inescapable universal God will not leave any of us to live by bread alone, or by ourselves alone, though we sometimes would flee Him and shut Him out of our lives if we really could. God may allow illness, death, sorrow, and misery to reign throughout His good earth, but He does not allow them to reign and rule out His good will and everlasting love. This is not because God is cruel, my friend, but because He is kind and perfect beyond our finite understanding and our little human ways of acting, talking, and thinking. God acts as the Sovereign of His created world and life through all reality by now known and now unknown causes and effects. God's Kingdom will win. It is forever, and not for a moment or just for our own lifetime.

"God, I admit, often seems to work impersonally through His universe and among all His children; but He actually knows and treats us all equally as persons, and not as robots or things. Because He really is God, He never gives us freedom to change the past. Even God cannot change the past, but He can change us no matter what our present fortunes and condition are. God leaves us free, more than we often are willing to believe, to help change our present and future courses of life—and those of our loved ones—by His grace. When we human beings suffer, God suffers too. He enters into our sufferings and agonies with understanding, love, and patience. We human beings may give up, or give other human beings up. But God never does. Nor does He ever regard any human being as utterly hopeless and beyond repair, if it takes forever for God to reclaim him. You want to be a co-worker with God, don't you? I am sure that He will help you through your faith and co-operation. My friend, your cause is God's also."

At times in this sharing, I confess: "Yes, there was a tragic yet rewarding time when I thought God was cruel to me, too. I remember beating my head, pulling my hair, and screaming at God behind the doors of two mental hospitals. I hated God for being what I thought was so inhuman to me. God let me pound away at myself and at the walls of my rooms, and at His infinite wisdom, honor, and glory. That did not change or hurt God one bit, only me. However, out of this personal hate came love, out of this misery came joy, out of this helplessness came God's help. Into this self-created Hellhole of suspicion, despair, and depression came a ladder from Heaven. I was too blinded by my own confusion to see for myself and to find God's ladder. In His own good time and wiser ways, God Himself came down that ladder, which I could not climb, at first, without the help of others. God revealed Himself, and carried me back to the world of reality and finally replaced me in His fold. I was lost, and He found me. This was not my will, but His. I was unlovely, but His love abided. I was untruthful, but He was truth. I was a minister with no local ministry; God has given me now a parish without boundaries. This is why you are in my office and sharing your problems with me today, my friend. Except for God, I would not be here. Except for God's Church you would not be here."

Another group of religiously upset people who come to me ask, "Isn't God punishing me for some 'secret sin'?" And others, with apparently the opposite problem, but actually the same one basically, inquire, "Isn't God planning this illness for some higher purpose that we don't know about yet?"

I point out that many people believe that God singles out their husband, wife, child, or parent to punish somebody else—or them—for some "secret" or "unpardonable sin." I testify: "God is not man-centered or man-controlled. But He is not inhuman, as some think, either. I admit that there is no escaping the chain reactions which are sometimes let loose to plague individual and family happiness, and which spring from the sinfulness of mankind or from sins of some individuals at times. But sin is not that simple. Nor does God rule His universe as though its whole purpose were to center upon one family or individual, either to dignify him or to get revenge upon him for anyone's or everyone's sins. All of us are sinners, equally, before God in a profound sense. All individuals, nations, and races embrace sin—whether we are aware of it or not—in false and selfish pride, in secret and public cravings to take the place of God or to possess God's infinite power and wisdom, and in our own illusions of self-sufficiency. Actually, we are all equal before God both in our distance from Him and in our own sinfulness and human limits; but also, in our infinite worth to God as persons who are His own children. We are all equally God's own people. God shares His judgments, love, and mercy equally. God is not partial, nor a player of favorites with any special moral or spiritual exemptions or privileges."

I also stress: "We simply don't know enough yet about mental and emotional illnesses to understand why all of them occur. But we have long known that they cannot be blamed upon God. When the Church used to teach that all illnesses and diseases, both physical and mental, were the results of the direct will and whim of God because of His displeasure against certain individuals or groups of people, the Church superstitiously prevented the development of both medical and mental sciences and benevolent practices for too many centuries. But in the long run the Church got a better understanding of God's love and will through the Bible and human experience. Christianity finally pioneered in establishing hospitals and in sending doctors and nurses all over the world. Until the leaders of Christian faith quit thinking that all suffering was the detailed plan and will of God, little was done to help any seriously sick persons to get well and be restored to society. The very idea of such help seemed sacrilegious to those who did not really know God-in-Christ better or who did not realize that Jesus Himself was called the 'Good Physician' in fulfilling God's purpose to save and heal all mankind. During those terrible centuries, suffering and sick people were thought to have deserved every pain, misery, and disease at the hand of Almighty God. All this is different now to anyone who approaches the Scriptures with the spirit and mind of the prophets and of Jesus Christ."

Sometimes I nail down these truths with this story about Mr. Harvey Harris, one of my own congregation. After I returned from my own hospitalization, he had to have a leg amputated because of diabetes. I say: "This was not caused because Mr. Harris had sinned any more grievously than most men who still have their two legs or good health. In fact, his whole life and faith were transformed long before his operation—in 1953, before I cracked up. He had been a 'wino'—one of the most difficult kinds of alcoholic to reclaim— before he first came to me about it. When he gave up drinking, he vitally accepted God through Christ in his own life. I know that his repentant, changed, and inspiring Christian life was a wonderful, humble, and holy influence upon numbers of people. He was happy and prayerful. But God did not prevent him from losing his leg later. Nor did God cause him to lose his leg. When Harvey lost his leg, his faith and tender understanding of God's will and of other human beings' handicaps and illnesses increased even beyond my prayers and hopes. Mr. Harris does not think that God is cruel, but now gratefully witnesses to his own growing faith in God's goodness to him through this tragic experience. Harvey helps troubled and handicapped people today as few could because he personally knows that God is not cruel. Would you like to meet him?"

I often repeat this true story to those who anxiously ask me:

"Isn't prayer enough? If one has enough faith, won't God cure him without the help of hospitals, doctors, and psychiatrists? Can't the Church do the job without science and medicine. Didn't Jesus say that faith can move mountains?"

I usually answer: "Yes, Jesus prayed as no one else ever has. His is the kind of faith that is good enough and great enough to help us all endure and transcend pain, suffering, illness, or death. The Cross of Christ witnesses to this truth. Yes, indeed, faith can and does move mountains, and literally does so today, through those who also believe in God's law and order in the natural world enough to learn how to apply this divine truth through engineering and scientific discoveries. And faith and prayer help many hospitals and specialists today to assist patients to get well, too. People are always praying for those who are mentally ill. Prayers help in ways that we cannot always fathom—in God's own complex ways and through the depths of human beings. But there is no substitute for God's wisdom, care, and help through the media of doctors, psychiatrists, mental hospitals, and technical aids and treatments which God has made possible to help mend untold numbers of broken lives and shattered minds. God, in His own infinite resource and love, has ways—some long known and some still undisclosed to mankind— of healing the sick and relieving suffering. But God always works through nature and through people and their cultures. In fact, God is so merciful and generous that many people who never pray and who are not religious or good or pure are blessed by God and made well. However, healthy prayer can speed up and deepen recoveries from all illnesses, physical and mental. Our job is not to pray less, but to pray more. At the same time we must cooperate more fully with every good cause and every helpful person whom God allows to serve so briefly on His good earth—including those in hospitals and laboratories."

Sometimes I frankly tell such questioners: "I don't know what the Church and modern Christians could do today in our complex society and machine age without the aid of modern science, specialists, and hospitals for the mentally and emotionally ill. Some of these practitioners and institutions are deeply religious; many are not. Whenever the Church in the past has tried to stifle the pioneers of human knowledge and social betterment, it has imprisoned the minds and souls of men by its own self-idolatry and rebellion against God's Word. I believe that God often works and speaks through so-called secular movements and causes to help even the Church understand His will and purpose to help save and heal all mankind. In fact, through modern science and research—some facets of which are more distinctly nonreligious than others—the Church has learned better how to use and understand its own Scriptures, history, and the world-wide and universal dimensions of its faith and works to serve Jesus Christ in His mission among peoples of all races, classes, conditions, and nations."

In any case, I always insist to those who want to tempt God by using faith and prayer alone: "For you to expect your prayers or those of a priest, minister, or rabbi to cure a profoundly critical mental and emotional illness without the aid of any science or technically skilled help is like trying to broadjump the Atlantic Ocean in one hop on prayer and faith alone. Have you considered the possible fact that you are tempted to use the forms of prayer as magic and man-made hocus-pocus? Are you sure that you grasp yet what real Christian prayer is? Would you like to discuss prayer more fully with me? Do you want me to give you some Bible passages about prayer to take home and study?"

Frequently I suggest to such religiously disturbed persons this kind of outlook: "How would you like to discover that God's grace through Christ really is sufficient for your moral and mental needs in this personal crisis? If you think that God is so cruel as to single out one individual or family for such punishment, do you believe that God is good? Why does the same God who allows innocent children to die before they learn to talk or crawl allow the self-styled 'pious' hypocrites and selfish screwballs to live and 'flourish like a green bay tree'? Can we ever fathom God's ultimate justice, which is beyond complete human understanding—yet within the reach of us all—until we accept His perfect love and mercy, transcending ours? When we cannot face ourselves and our own human limitations squarely, we cannot see God's face clearly even in Jesus Christ or in the redemptive work of the prophets, the apostles, and the saints of all ages and religions.

"Yet prayer, faith, and the Church often can help to reveal and alleviate many mental and emotional illnesses in a unique way. I found this to be true during my own illness and recovery. And it is just as true today in our pioneer work toward the prevention of such diseases. These diseases are much easier to help prevent than they are to cure or endure."

I have seen persons whose dreams and lives have been broken and shattered avoid stepping too far over the thin line between normal and abnormal health. There are untold millions of them today. I have met my fair share of them in my office, in chapels, in cars, and in homes—hearing their confessions and sharing their prayers and confusion. Nervous, shaking, and profoundly disturbed to the point of considering suicide or murder, they have found a new faith, a new hope, and a mission bigger than themselves and their complex personal problems. And I have seen many rise up from prayer and go forth without wavering in the direction of such illnesses again.

I shall never forget the struggle to increase my own faith as the problems of readjustments became more complex. The event that helped me the most was my reading of a sermon by Dr. Harry Emerson Fosdick in the *Christian Century* "Pulpit." Only one paragraph astonished me. For two decades I had read too much from his pen to be surprised at anything in his wisdom and realism about human needs. But this paragraph shared his faith about what an early critical nervous breakdown did to bless his own life and long ministry.

I had never known that Fosdick had had that experience. But I had wondered why he seemed to understand the inner problems of man and society so realistically. I had never been moved deeply by his theology. The thoughts of Professors Reinhold Niebuhr, Paul Tillich, Richard Niebuhr, Robert L. Calhoun, Emil Brunner, John Bennett, and others were more challenging for my life and faith. However, in his personal story Dr. Fosdick claimed that out of his severe nervous breakdown came his early book *The Meaning of Prayer*. He claimed that he could never have written that book had he not had a breakdown.

During my first few months back from the hospital, I was disappointed because I tired too quickly while reading the works of my favorite theologians. But I could easily read biographies and less complex expressions of faith from the lives of some great Christians of ages past and of today. Among the most helpful books were those by Dr. Fosdick. As I reread them, they were lamps unto my feet.

My greatest test for progress in more difficult reading and self-study came early when I was asked to write a review of Reinhold Niebuhr's *The Self and the Drama of History*. For weeks I could read only a few pages at a time. Finally, to my joy, I could read a chapter at a sitting. Then I improved so that I could handle the entire book in the same stride that I would have done before my breakdown. This was a personal victory, but the book meant more than that to me, for it spoke to my condition and to my deepest inner moral and spiritual hungers. It told of every man's threefold dialogues which are inescapable and universal: between himself and God, between himself and society, and between himself and himself.

Later, I reread Dr. Fosdick's book *Living Under Tension*. My ministry and life were strengthened by another reference to his early breakdown in the ministry in his sermon "Essential Elements in a Vital Christian Experience." I asked myself, "Why didn't I notice that when I read the book years ago?" Before I read the sermon, I had been challenged by his account of how a man in great despair visited him, reminding him of his own great personal despair long ago. When the guest began to tell Dr. Fosdick how he felt, the understanding minister interrupted, "Don't tell me how you feel; let me tell you!" Then Dr. Fosdick drew for the troubled man "a blueprint of all that was going on in his mind and heart." In amazement the man said, "My God, how did you know that?"

Fosdick explained that they were on common ground because they could not help saying "we" and "our." Fosdick claimed that such persons were on his own "wave length."* Since 1954 I have discovered that he was right. We who have been critically troubled or ill are on the wave lengths of untold numbers of persons in our generation.

The favorite text which I share in my own life with the troubled and with those who are on my own wave length is from Romans 8:28. Before the Revised Standard versions of the Bible put this verse in up-to-date English, it read as though God were cruel, partial, and childish in His discipline and care for many individuals. But in its original New Testament meaning, the verse now rings with common sense and abiding realism: "We know that in everything God works for good *with* those who love him, who are called to serve him." God makes it rain upon the just and the unjust, and upon all sorts and conditions of human beings alike. But he especially can bless and work most effectively with those who work *with* Him. Our task is to cooperate in response to His good will, and to love God and others regardless of what happens in our own little individual lives and to our minds and health.

God does not directly will everything that happens to an individual, but He does provide guidance and strength sufficient for any

* *Living Under Tension* (New York, Harper and Brothers, 1941), p. 91.

individual's needs in any situation. But an individual must do his own part to give God a chance to find him when he and others have trampled the image of God, whose stamp is upon the nature of all mankind.

In sharing my faith that God is not cruel, I keep on my desk one verse of a hymn which meant much to some of us patients as we sang it together in the chapel at Dix Hill. This verse of the hymn "Love of God," written about 1050 by Meir Ben Isaac Neherai, was found scribbled by an unknown patient on the wall of his locked room in a mental institution:

> "Could we with ink the ocean fill,
>   And were the sky of parchment made:
> Were every stalk on earth a quill,
>   And every man a scribe by trade,
> To write the Love of God above
>   Would drain the oceans dry.
> Nor could the scroll contain the whole
>   Though stretched from sky to sky."*

It would have been worth any kind of illness and confinement for a person to have experienced such faith in God! But a man does not have to become mentally or emotionally ill to respond to God with such superb faith. He has only to keep his needed distance from God, and at the same time love God's nearness in every sick and well person on the face of this mysterious earth.

---

* From "The Love of God," copyright 1917; copyright renewed 1945 by Nazarene Publishing House. Used by permission.